THE MODERN SAINTS

THE MODERN SAINTS

PORTRAITS AND REFLECTIONS ON THE SAINTS

EDITED AND ILLUSTRATED BY

GRACIE MORBITZER

CONVERGENT BOOKS
NEW YORK

Published in the United States by Convergent Books, an imprint of Random House, a division of Penguin Random House LLC, New York.

Grateful acknowledgment is made to Jessica Gerhardt for permission to reprint lyrics from "Keep It Simple," copyright © 2022 by Jessica Gerhardt. Reprinted by permission.

Contributor credits appear on pages 300–301.

The following are never-before-seen portraits: The New Eve, St. Dominic, St. Brigid, Sts. Priscilla and Aquila, St. Óscar Romero, St. Dismas, St. Peregrine, St. Zoe, St. Simeon Stylites the Younger, St. Madeleine Sophie Barat, St. Kevin, St. Zélie, St. Martha, Stella Maris, St. Catherine of Bologna, St. Mark Ji Tianxiang, St. Olympias, St. Junia, St. Martin of Tours, and St. Elizabeth of Hungary.

Hardback ISBN 978-0-593-44444-3
Ebook ISBN 978-0-593-44445-0

PRINTED IN CHINA ON ACID-FREE PAPER

crownpublishing.com

2 4 6 8 9 7 5 3 1

First Edition

Book design by Elizabeth Rendfleisch

Humanity, take a good look at yourself. Inside, you've got heaven and earth, and all of creation. You're a world—everything is hidden in you.

—Hildegard of Bingen, *Causae et Curae*

AUTHOR'S NOTE

With justice, truth, and love being virtues held in the highest regard by the saints, it is the least I could do to acknowledge the context in which this work was created.

I want to take the opportunity to address the centuries of violence and cultural erasure that Christians and the Catholic Church in particular have enacted upon Indigenous cultures through missionary work and colonization. I condemn these evils and am committed to honesty, transparency, and accountability when sharing the history of the Church and its members. I am dedicated to understanding the ongoing impact of these sins and working toward ending mindsets and practices that perpetuate them.

While this book contains essays from all over the United States and Canada, I want to acknowledge that the land on which this book was compiled and edited is the homeland of the Miami, Shawnee, Wyandot, Delaware, and other nations. This land was seized by the federal government with the Treaty of Greenville in 1795 and resulted in the forced removal of tribes in 1830. I want to recognize the enduring legacy of the Indigenous people of this land and of all the lands in which these reflections were written.

CONTENTS

Introduction xiii

THE NEW EVE—BY MORGAN STREHLOW 2

ST. ELIZABETH ANN SETON—BY MAGGIE PHILPOT 8

DOMINIC DE GUZMAN—
BY RENÉE DARLINE RODEN 14

ST. TERESA OF AVILA—BY MADISON CHASTAIN 20

ST. BRIGID—KERRY CAMPBELL 26

OUR LADY UNDOER OF KNOTS—
BY MARIE HEIMANN 30

STS. PRISCILLA AND AQUILA—
BY INDIA JADE MCCUE 36

ST. CYPRIAN—BY MARCIE ALVIS WALKER 42

ST. IGNATIUS OF LOYOLA—BY FR. JAMES MARTIN 48

STS. PERPETUA AND FELICITY—BY SARA BILLUPS 54

ST. MARY MACKILLOP—BY ISABEL MORBITZER 60

ST. ÓSCAR ROMERO—BY CAMERON BELLM 64

ST. JOHN—BY EVE TUSHNET 70

ST. DISMAS—BY ELISE CRAWFORD GALLAGHER 76

ST. BERNADETTE—BY JESSICA GERHARDT 82

ST. BRENDAN—BY SARAH QUINT 88

ST. HILDEGARD OF BINGEN—
BY MEGHAN TSCHANZ 94

ST. PEREGRINE—BY ABBY ELLIS 100

ST. ZOE—BY CARA MEREDITH 106

MADONNA AND CHILD—BY CAMILLE HERNANDEZ 110

ST. SIMEON STYLITES THE YOUNGER—
BY GRACIE MORBITZER 116

ST. MADELEINE SOPHIE BARAT—
BY LETICIA OCHOA ADAMS 122

STS. SERGIUS AND BACCHUS—BY THEO SWINFORD 128

ST. KEVIN—BY TRACY BALZER 132

ST. PAUL—BY RYAN J. PELTON 138

ST. JOHN THE BAPTIST—BY BOND STRONG 144

ST. JUAN DIEGO—BY KARLA MENDOZA ARANA 148

ST. ZÉLIE—BY CLAIRE SWINARSKI 154

ST. CHRISTOPHER—BY GRACIE MORBITZER 158

ST. ANNE—BY ERIN S. LANE 162

ST. MARTHA—BY SHANNON W. SCHMIDT 168

ST. EDITH STEIN—BY CORYNNE STARESINIC 174

ST. JANE FRANCES DE CHANTAL—
BY STINA KIELSMEIER-COOK 180

STELLA MARIS—BY NYA ABERNATHY 184

ST. MONICA—BY TSH OXENREIDER 190

ST. TERESA OF CALCUTTA—BY RAKHI MCCORMICK 196

ST. LUKE—BY SOLOME HAILE 202

ST. CATHERINE OF BOLOGNA—BY JUSTINA KOPP 208

ST. MARK JI TIANXIANG—BY BETH JENKINS ERNEST 214

ST. THÉRÈSE OF LISIEUX—BY JENNY NUTZMAN 220

OUR LADY OF VICTORY—BY ALEX GOTAY, JR. 226

ST. KATERI TEKAKWITHA—BY KIRBY HOBERG 232

ST. OLYMPIAS—BY RÉNEE DARLINE RODEN 238

THE MYRRHBEARERS—BY LAURA KELLY FANUCCI 244

ST. JUNIA—BY JENNY BOOTH POTTER 250

ST. MARTIN OF TOURS—BY JULIE CANLIS 256

ST. ELIZABETH OF HUNGARY—
BY KRISTIN THOMAS SANCKEN 262

ST. CATHERINE OF ALEXANDRIA—
BY CHRISTENA CLEVELAND, PHD 268

ST. DYMPHNA—BY D. L. MAYFIELD 274

OUR LADY OF GUADALUPE—BY VICTORIA MASTRANGELO 280

THE VISITATION—BY KELLY SANKOWSKI 286

THE HOLY FAMILY—BY ERICA TIGHE CAMPBELL 290

Acknowledgments 295

Bibliography 297

Notes 298

List of Contributors 300

DIVINE MERCY

ARTIST'S STATEMENT—Since this is the first icon I ever painted, it's a little different from the others. Keeping Jesus in a simple white T-shirt, though, was the decision that brought about all of this.

INTRODUCTION

BY GRACIE MORBITZER

The first time I was in the room for an impromptu "Christianity bash session" in college, in a class, not a dorm room, by the way, a part of me shrunk, shriveled up, and assumed the fetal position inside. So much of the discussion felt like a personal attack that it took another year or two before I could go back over the arguments (which I had plenty more opportunities to hear, by then) and unpack them. I realized they were more about attacking the actions of people claiming an identity as Christian—or using that label as an excuse—and that most of the arguments were actually things I agreed with, too. *I* had been deeply wounded by Christians in the name of Christianity. *I* had been excluded by youth groups. *I* had been spiritually abused by those in positions of religious authority. *I* had been told hurtful things "in the name of Love," *too*.

But there was still within me a feeling of sadness about this. I had grown up in the faith, and I honestly loved and truly believed many aspects of it. It saddened me that the people around me had been so vehemently against it, when I found it could be so beautiful and healing. But how could I blame them? In the name of this religion, they had been kicked out of their homes, had their identities laughed at or labeled "evil" and "wrong," and had been judged harshly all their lives. I supposed the only difference for me—and the only reason I might still hold on to this faith at all—was that despite my own trauma in the name of religion, I had at least a few Christians in my life who were genuinely loving and caring, and they modeled how their own faith could never allow or condone the hatred conveyed by so many others. Some of these Christians were my family or teachers, but some were the saints.

I have always loved hearing stories and learning about different time periods and places. Therefore, when I was growing up in Catholic school, saint projects were always my favorite assignments. I loved getting to choose someone with such a human story who might remind me of someone in my own life and give me a completely new perspective on Jesus and the Church. Each saint is so different, with their own skills, talents, and passions, and discovering that there is a saint for basically anything a person could go through just felt so welcoming and so inclusive to me.

This idea of examining the saints, I realized, is exactly what I needed to bring to my college situation. Not only to welcome the folks who'd been hurt by the Church—to see the hope that could come from learning about stories similar to theirs, but also to show members of the Church—the ones who had done the hurting—that they might, in fact, be casting out and abusing future saints.

To do this, I wanted to share the stories of the saints, but how would I get anyone to even want to engage with them?

Well, I supposed, in the way that people had been doing for years, through the one thing I knew I could do at least relatively well: art.

How much more inviting could it be to someone on the outside of the Church to see someone within the Church who is so revered and either looks like them or has a story just like theirs? And on the flip side, how convincing for someone within the Church to see an image of a beloved saint that might look like someone they had recently written off or judged? For everyone, how powerful would it be to see the saints, with so much history and fame and holiness, look just like them or someone they know?

For the longest time, the whitewashing of the saints as portrayed in ancient European icons has angered me. I hate seeing the diverse Church—as diverse as it could get based on the people Jesus was involved with—reduced to a bunch of images of elderly white people with no expressions. Now, I absolutely love traditional iconography, but it, along with European medieval and Renaissance religious paintings, has overrun the popular art catalog by being featured in prestigious museums, with copies in homes, churches, and public spaces. As with so many other aspects of culture, the

Western forms are still, destructively, often the only ones embraced as serious and noteworthy. This leads to the fact that our most easily accessible images of saints are ones in which they are incorrectly portrayed in skin tone and features. Therefore, I knew I had so much research ahead of me when I sought to finally correct the looks and ages of the saints. This effort was most important to me not only for its historical value but for its social impact, too. Studies indicate that if a person sees the people they believe to be most holy and powerful (God, Jesus, the saints, et cetera) as white, then they will be bound to subconsciously believe that the most holy and powerful people in society will be white too, no matter their own race or background. I wanted to do something about the injustice of erasing the perfect way God made someone, be it skin color, features, ability, or style.

In my research I did learn one thing from the Renaissance paintings, which was how impactful it must have been for those communities to see Jesus and the saints wearing current Renaissance clothing and inhabiting the spaces of their daily life. It was one way these paintings captured how real the legendary people were—how they were engaged in the same everyday tasks we are, how they struggled with the same human issues, how they had their own style, emotions, personalities, just like we do.

One of my favorite parts of the project came about by accident, and really was what brought about all of these ideas. At a flea market, I stumbled upon two pieces of wood that reminded me of the wood of ancient icons. Though the pieces I found had kitten and butterfly images on them with cheesy quotes, I thought I could give them a new life. I painted Jesus and Mary (which I later learned is a traditional way to begin as an iconographer, so that fact just added to my confidence in the project) and then decided to add St. Genevieve, my Confirmation saint. I liked the way the wood looked and realized that if I were to paint more saints on repurposed wood pieces, this element would be a metaphor for the saints themselves. Wood found in various states, shapes, forms, and purposes, with tears, breaks, and imprints from past uses, could be transformed and then revered. I chose to leave some of the wood's texture and damage visible, however, because these people weren't made perfect when they became saints—they were still themselves, with their past wounds and flaws as part of the texture of their lives.

Since I wanted to paint the saints in the same vein as more traditional iconography, I decided to include solid-color backgrounds, as well as each saint's name in the Greek found on the ancient icons. I chose to mimic poses, colors, and other details of specific saints from ancient icons as another nod to tradition. I also included symbols that represent parts of each saint's story or patronage—but in ways that fit with their modern style: T-shirt designs, jewelry, tattoos, and hairpieces—rather than portraying the saints as simply holding an entire church in their hands or bearing the instruments of their death. This subtle change, I hoped, would also make these people more accessible. Ancient art that shows the saints in the midst of terrible torture can be terrifying to those unacquainted with the tradition, and might lead someone to believe that they could never be like the saints because they would never be able to endure those things. But the saints were normal people who likely had similar thoughts. That's one aspect of the saints' stories that I find more important now than in past centuries, since being martyred for the faith is no longer as common in the Western world.

Since painting my first 3 icons, I have added over 150 saints to my collection. Requests by friends and family jump-started sales of my paintings at my college art fair, which led to me creating a website, which led to individual commissions, a full-time job, and now, this book. I still cannot believe I am here—this little side project has become something so much bigger than I could have ever imagined. I have learned so much about so many incredible people—both saints and fans—and the small change this work has been able to bring about convinces me that it is worth it to continue despite the hate and criticism that does, inevitably, come my way. The whole point of an icon is to deepen a viewer's ideas about and understanding of the person depicted. The icon is meant to act as a visual form of prayer and contemplation. And yet, it is still too much of a new thing for many people to process, and their experience views it negatively. I can only hope that like many of the saints, my work will one day come to be understood. The awareness I aim to bring with this project is one I believe our world desperately needs—but luckily, I am not alone in this work.

Thanks to many different writers and artists, fifty of whom are included in this collection, the process of this project has been, more than anything, a learning experience for me. My ideas about faith have changed drastically since I began because of my interaction with these fellow sojourners. Their words and images have allowed my ideas to expand, grow, and become more loving, more justice-hungry, more understanding, and more open every day. These writers have been doing faithful work since long before I ever had an idea for my art, and they know, imagine, and understand more than I ever could. It is because of them that my art is possible and accepted in this world even the slightest bit. They are changing hearts and minds, healing wounds, and bettering this world. They are holding us all accountable and exposing truth.

I can't wait for you to meet these saints, and the ones they have written about, too.

It is the greatest honor I could ever have to find their words paired with my work. In each section, you will find an icon with a brief artist's statement, a short biography of the saint, and an author's reflection on why this saint is still relevant today or what we can learn from the person depicted. Each essay is followed by a prayer to help you reflect on the saint's story and ideas, and perhaps guide you on a path for the rest of the day or week. With fifty-two essays, this book can be used as a weekly meditation piece throughout a year, or it can be read through at once like a traditional book. You will find how much we have in common with these figures from history, and what part of the story of the Christian faith they bring to the table. You will find, ultimately, just how much the saints were like you—and how you can be like them. No matter your position on faith, how you may have hurt or been hurt in the past, I hope reading about the humanity of the saints can bring you healing, empathy, hope, more questions, and a place to start on this journey.

—Gracie Morbitzer, artist and owner, The Modern Saints

THE MODERN SAINTS

THE NEW EVE

FEAST: **JANUARY 1**

MARIAN DEVOTION

THE SHORT STORY—Mary's title "The New Eve" is one of the oldest we have for her, signifying her necessary participation in the story of Jesus's redemption. In the second century, St. Justin Martyr was one of the first to draw the parallel between Mary and Eve, just as one is drawn between Jesus and Adam. St. Irenaeus also wrote of this parallel, comparing Eve's disobedience to Mary's obedience, and Mary's faith to Eve's lack of it. Tertullian later continued this idea, comparing Mary's belief in an angel to Eve's belief in the serpent, and saying that Eve gave birth to a son who would kill, while Mary gave birth to one who would be killed. St. Jerome in the fourth century simply wrote that death came through Eve while life came through Mary. St. Augustine also used this title "The New Eve" to prove that both male and female bodies are pleasing to God because Mary's divine role was just as necessary as Jesus's. Symbolism around Eve often involves lush, fertile fruits of the garden, and though she and Adam brought death and Original Sin, Mary reclaimed that fertility and lushness of life for us.

ARTIST'S STATEMENT—Since I began this project, the portrayal of Mary during her pregnancy has been one of my most requested images. The title *The New Eve,* I believe, is the best fit for this image, with its indication of fertility and vibrancy. She is gardening, with her watering can overflowing as a reference to her other, similar title: "Life-giving Spring." She also has in her pocket a snakeskin and a broken chain—symbols of her liveliness's power over death and the freedom it gives us. She holds and wears flowers and fruit—more symbols of life, growth, and abundance. Her pose gives a sense of her enjoyment of this bounty, while her face shows a gentleness and peace.

BY MORGAN STREHLOW

The liminality between Eden and Bethlehem leaves me with a delicate belief that often feels like holding faith in one hand and doubt in the other.

My curiosities are big and my hunger for knowledge is great, but the answers I have been given are more mysterious than they are mitigating.

I make a pretty good devil's advocate if I say so myself.

Did God really say that? (Gen. 3:1 NIV)

I often wonder how Eve must have felt, on her knees outside of the garden, desperately grasping for the only home she had ever had, unknowingly striving for something she would never again touch or taste. I wonder how long she might have hovered there at the gates of Eden, begging God for all to be made good again, to be made right, to be made perfect. I wonder what it was like to feel shame, regret, sadness, and fear for the very first time.

I wonder what happened between Genesis 3 and Genesis 4—in between the garden and Eve's new life as mother of all the living. Did the memory of what had once been very good and without sin remain with her? Or was it overcome by the lingering memories of birth pangs as she mothered children who would kill and who would be killed?

We learn in Genesis 5 that Adam lived to be 930 years old, but we do not get more about the life of Eve. Did she become a bitter woman, always ruminating on what could have been? Did she withdraw from her family? Was she lonely? Or was she able to forgive herself and live a life of love and delight, knowing God was still the good father who walked with her in the garden?

Did Eve remain curious and adventurous? Did she still talk to her animals? Or did she wilt away, hiding in the shadows, disempowered and deflated in a silent prison of shame?

I feel a kindredness with Eve on the days when belief becomes a hard-fought battle to be won rather than a shelter that protects from harm, aching for some certainty that God is here with me, still.

When I close my eyes, I hope for Kingdom Come, and in my prayerful imagination I picture Eve and me returning to the garden in all of its lushness and goodness, where our heads are lifted, our fragile faith is restored, and our belovedness is known.

Greetings, favored woman! The Lord is with you. (Luke 1:28 NLT)

When Mary opened her eyes to a messenger from God, she welcomed the Christ into her very womb.

She said, "May it be done to me according to your word" (Luke 1:38 HCSB). I wonder how many minutes passed before Mary spoke these words aloud, giving her young body—her whole life—to God's saving work. Did she tremble as the sentence left her lips? Or did she feel the Peace her body was now growing inside?

I marvel at this mysterious mother of Jesus, whom a spirit-filled Elizabeth called "blessed among women" (Luke 1:42 NLT) because of her remarkable belief that God would fulfill his promises in her. For when the rest of humanity perpetually failed to take God at his word, suffering from generational trauma and sin, retreating from the other and resorting to individualism, Mary believed—on our behalf—what God said to be true, and in doing so, she charted a path toward hope, toward peace, toward Love.

The promised one was on his way.

When hope is hard to come by and skepticism creeps in, I look to an expectant Mary and cling to her belief, following her all the way to Bethlehem. And, just before my waning faith dries up, the breaking of water brings an end to the drought, and the arrival of Jesus Christ makes a way out of the wilderness.

Mary points us to Jesus.
Jesus points us to Love.
And Love points us home.

Thy kingdom come, thy will be done in earth, as it is in heaven. (Matt. 6:10 KJV)

I want to believe that belief in God—however big or small it may be—is enough, and that may be true. But I can't help but wonder if belief is not the finish line to salvation but rather the starting line.

Will I have the courage to respond to God's leading, echoing Mary's obedience? Or will I remain a devil's advocate, resigning myself to a self-indulgent pursuit of knowledge rather than the pursuit of peace? The tension between personal autonomy and choosing to follow God toward our collective liberation is palpable. I'm pacing in this liminal space between my desire for self-protection, for power, for control, and my desire for Kingdom Come.

Just as Mary carried and gave life to the Son of God, we are invited to consider that which is being conceived in our own lives and hearts. As bearers of God's image and vessels of the Kingdom Come, may we each consciously choose to carry the Holy One and, like Mary, give birth to Hope, Peace, Joy, and Love for this weary world.

PRAYER

O God, Creator of our wombs
Creator of our bleeding, birthing bodies
Creator of the mysteries we carry within

May your peace surpass our understanding
May our laboring make way for your Love

Help us to be generous with our faith, when we have it
Help us to be gentle with ourselves, when we don't

When we find ourselves in the in-between space
May we find you in the unlikely places
Through unsuspecting wayfinders of your Love
Pointing us in the way of your glory.

MORGAN STREHLOW is a writer, editor, and book coach who loves to come alongside others to help cultivate and communicate powerful stories that can change the world. She is also the host of *Sanctuary Woman,* a podcast that centers ecumenicism, spiritual hospitality, contemplative activism, and shame-free sexual formation. Strehlow is married to her former college tennis teammate and teammate for life, Sean, and is mother to their son, Seth.

ST. ELIZABETH ANN SETON

ARTIST'S STATEMENT—I imagine Elizabeth as a bit of a quiet soul, maybe a little shy, especially after all she endured. Her glasses are a symbol of her valuing of education, and her sweater a protection from her losses. Her eyes, though, look bravely toward the good that she was able to do.

BORN: **AUGUST 28, 1774**
DIED: **JANUARY 4, 1821**
FEAST: **JANUARY 4**
PATRON OF TEACHERS, SCHOOLS, IN-LAWS, WIDOWS, LOSS OF PARENTS, LOSS OF CHILDREN, OPPOSITION OF CHURCH AUTHORITIES

THE SHORT STORY—Born at the beginning of the American Revolution, Elizabeth grew up in New York City. At nineteen, she married William Magee Seton. They had five children, and it is said that their marriage was an extremely happy and loving one. They lived on Wall Street, and Elizabeth continued doing what she had been taught and loved—traversing the city to care for the hungry, sick, and dying. Unfortunately, William's business failed, forcing him to declare bankruptcy, and as a result, William and Elizabeth lost their home and were forced to move in with Elizabeth's father. Shortly after, William was diagnosed with tuberculosis. Doctors prescribed a visit to a warmer climate, so William, Elizabeth, and their oldest daughter sailed to Italy, but William did not survive the journey. Elizabeth was heartbroken. Once she arrived in Italy, though, Elizabeth was exposed to the Catholic faith, and upon her return to New York, she converted. To support the family, Elizabeth began a school and taught there. Though she was in poor health, she moved to Maryland and began another school—this time, a free school for girls. She also established a religious order there to provide for the school and community. Her daughter Anna Maria died of tuberculosis in 1812, and her daughter Rebecca died in 1816.

BY MAGGIE PHILPOT

When I reflect on Elizabeth's life, I find myself asking, How much is one person to bear? And further, How did she bear it?

I remember vividly when I received the news that a young boy I had grown close to during a season spent abroad tested positive for HIV. Though he wasn't family and I hadn't known him long, my soul ached for him. I was filled with anger and grief, shaking my fist at a God who would allow this to happen to a young child. The anger stayed with me for a long time as I wrestled with the perpetual questions surrounding the problem of pain and the nature of God. But the thing is, there's no truly satisfying answer to suffering.

One of C. S. Lewis's greatest books (in my humble opinion) is *A Grief Observed,* which is not a treatise on the nature of suffering, but an honest wandering and stumbling through a very personal and very deep loss. In it he writes, "We were promised sufferings. They were part of the program. We were even told, 'Blessed are they that mourn,' and I accept it. I've got nothing that I hadn't bargained for. Of course it is different when the thing happens to oneself, not to others, and in reality, not imagination."[1]

Lewis himself finds the journey of loss to be a long and winding one, and one without a clear end. While grief may be a given in this broken world, the reality of it is messy, complex, and constant. How do we bear it?

I'm sure the suffering of St. Elizabeth was no less complex. Her own letters after her husband's death are striking in how they portray the steadfast nature of her faith. She wrote to Rebecca Seton that the loss of her husband "would be death to any one not supported by the Almighty Comforter, but his Mercy has supported, and still upholds, and in it alone I trust."[2] Yet at the same time, she writes that her "poor . . . heart was in the clouds roving after my William's soul and repeating 'my God you are my God,' and so I am now alone in the world with you and my little ones but you are my Father and doubly theirs."[3] How will she bear it?

As bearers of the prolonged burden of pain, we can become consumed by our suffering. We can allow that pain to become a black hole, sucking in what is good and lovely. This is both excruciatingly painful and easy to do. Or, as C. S. Lewis concluded, we can get on with what we know we should do. "I know the two great commandments,*" he wrote, "and I'd better get on with them." And that is precisely what St. Elizabeth Ann Seton did.

Another strong woman, Maya Angelou, wrote in *Letter to My Daughter,* "You may not control all the events that happen to you, but you can decide not to be reduced by them."[4] The many tragedies faced by Ms. Seton did change her in many ways, the most significant perhaps being her conversion to Catholicism. But instead of reducing her, these tragedies increased her stature. She faced a myriad of prejudices against Catholics in early-nineteenth-century America without cowering or complaining. She founded a free school that marks the start of parochial schools in the United States, formed the first religious sisterhood in the Americas, and left a legacy that has changed the lives of thousands for the better. This, I am convinced, was not in spite of her suffering, but because of it.

Over the years I have found that the hurts and losses I have experienced, if I can hang on and wrestle with them well, create fertile soil for greater empathy and greater kindness to bloom. Does it still hurt? Certainly. As I'm certain St. Elizabeth Ann Seton always felt the many losses of her own life. But in a world in which suffering is unavoidable, may we too ride out that suffering in all of its pain and find ourselves enlarged by it.

PRAYER

Lord God,

May whatever pain I experience open my eyes to the sufferings of others. May I grow larger out of my own trials,

* To love the Lord your God and love your neighbor as yourself.

finding in them a new strength and a new purpose. And may I too hold fast to my vessel of faith through the waves of tragedy and sorrow.

Amen

MAGGIE PHILPOT spends the majority of her time poorly managing her house, stumbling through a graduate program in writing, and making a fool of herself to make her two young boys laugh. But in every spare moment she plays in the land of words and stories. She has written an Advent book for families called *God Is Coming* but spends most of her writing life in the realm of middle-grade novels and poetry.

ART REFLECTION—I am hoping you can tell from this icon that I think in this day and ge, Dominic would be the guy who just sold all his stuff to go on a soul-searching road rip (with pit stops to help anyone and everyone he comes across who needs it), looking or a purpose and taking all opportunities along the way. He might also be a NASA fan, nd, in this image, he is gazing at the stars with his dog after setting up camp for the ight. He has space-themed and Dominican patches on his very spacesuit-like metallic acket, as well as a hat (from his travels) featuring a patch of the Dominican Republic's lag. His dog carries the torch (flashlight) by which he was destined to bring a little light

BORN: **AUGUST 8, 1170**

DIED: **AUGUST 6, 1221**

FEAST: **AUGUST 8**

PATRON OF ASTRONOMERS, THE DOMINICAN REPUBLIC, THE DOMINICAN ORDER

THE SHORT STORY—Dominic was born around the year 1170 in the city of Caleruega in the Castile region of Spain. Legend says that Dominic's barren mother prayed for a son and saw a vision of a dog with a torch in its mouth, setting the world on fire. Thus, her son came to be named Dominic because the vision was of the Domini Canis—Dog of the Lord.

Dominic was ordained a priest in his mid-twenties and began working as a cathedral canon, ministering to different parishes. Dominic's life changed forever when he went on a diplomatic trip to Denmark with Diego d'Azevedoto, the Bishop of Osma. On their way, they passed through southern France, where they encountered the Cathars, a heretical sect of Christians that practiced severe asceticism, denied the goodness of the body, and lived in celibate convents. Dominic felt a surge of love in his heart for these Christians and the misery and suffering their ideas caused them, so he dedicated his life to preaching to them.

In 1213 Dominic petitioned Pope Innocent III for permission to start the order of preachers, and they founded their first monastery around 1216 in Toulouse, the heart of the Cathars' territory.

After Dominic's death in 1221, the Dominicans spread across Europe by planting their convents near newly developed universities. The Dominican order is itself responsible for great institutions of learning and has given great minds to the Church, including several Doctors of the Church.

BY RENÉE DARLINE RODEN

History is alive with Christ. It is full of the movement of the Holy Spirit across the waters and the beating hearts of humans like you and me who have wondered how to love and live and how to carry on. The saints help us to see history as a story of the brave souls who responded to the real needs of their day. They show us that God is alive in our world, and they remind us that we can respond to the needs of our world as alertly and as creatively and fiercely as the saints did—as Christ did.

Dominic lived in what is often known as the Dark Ages. Traveling around Europe continually, preaching the truth relentlessly, he is said to have walked barefoot often, offering up his pain as a penance to save souls. When he encountered the Cathars, he dedicated his life to preaching to them. Also known as the Albigensians, or "pure ones," the Cathars believed that all flesh was of the devil and only that which was spiritual was of God. They denied the sacramentality of marriage and they lived in ascetic convents of men and women where they abstained from food and from sex.

The Cathars' denial of the goodness of our bodily flesh was a heresy because it denied the full reality of God's Incarnation. Dominic was known for his devotion to Mary, and he is often credited with the popularization of the rosary. Dominic's love for the rosary as a way to meditate on Christ's life emphasizes the incarnational aspect of the Catholic faith. The love of God is made known through the ordinary, fleshly lives of the virgin Mary and through the incarnate Christ.

St. Dominic's life inspires me with his unhesitating love for his fellow humans, his desire to lead them to the truth, and his love of learning the truth and preaching it. But even more than his words, it is his actions that motivate me. His poverty; his endless journeying about Europe, which wore him out; his penance; his tears in prayer for souls in need of salvation—his love speaks louder than any homily, letter, or sermon ever could.

We live in a world of words—our lives are lived on screens—we are often divorced, like the Albigensians, from the realities of our animal flesh. Marshall McLuhan, the Canadian media theorist, called natives of the digital age "disincarnate beings."[5]

Too often, Catholics police one another on saying the right things and thinking the right things rather than doing the right things. Dominic, a preacher of the truth, preached not just with his mouth or with his words but with his whole life. I find inspiration in Dominic to let my life speak, not only through words, but by letting the Truth take root in my body and truly change the way I live. Incarnation means we cannot know the truth unless we truly live it. So many of us—myself included—want to be great. I want to be famous, well-known, loved. But, I ask myself, what do I want to be known for?

Over the course of my three decades of living, as I have sifted through my motives and confronted the various parts of me that clamor for acclaim and affirmation, I have come to realize that true greatness is simply the quality and power of our love.

Dominic's greatness seems to be in his preaching, his magnetic influence, winning others over to "his side," or persuading others. But really, his greatness is in his commitment to loving the people in front of him—not hypothetical people I'll meet one day, but *these* people—this person—this homeless woman who smells so bad, my family member who pushes all my buttons, the partner or spouse who points out a failing. Or, to Dominic—this self-righteous Cathar, in their error. Can I love the real people around me, not the ideal people I'll love so well someday? Can I love them with my whole heart and soul, truly seeing Christ in them and honoring them with the gentleness, love, and care I crave from them?

Love delights in truth and the truth sets us free for love. Dominic saw that suffering could be remedied with the light of truth. To St. Dominic, the love of God truly was a light that shines into the darkness of the world, and the darkness could not and cannot overcome it.

No one may ever write a story about the moments that make us saints, no one will make podcasts, write books, or make movies about what will make us great. But it is the fierce, creative love inside of us that will quietly remake the world.

PRAYER

St. Dominic, whose love for learning has given the Church so many great minds aflame with love, and whose love for clarity of thought and God's creation has revealed to your fellow humans the things of Heaven, intercede for us to our mother Mary, that we may understand more and more fully the presence of God in our lives, and bear God's love into the world.

RENÉE DARLINE RODEN is a journalist and playwright from Minnesota. She currently lives at St. Francis Catholic Worker House in Chicago.

ST. TERESA OF AVILA

ARTIST'S STATEMENT—Despite all her suffering, Teresa valued joy. I wanted her to express that, as well as contentment, in this image. Despite her constant health and interpersonal battles, she did win out in the end. She was strong, intelligent, and holy, but she also found an importance in remaining womanly and feminine throughout her life.

BORN: **MARCH 28, 1515**

DIED: **OCTOBER 4, 1582**

FEAST: **OCTOBER 15**

PATRON OF HEADACHES, SEIZURES, SPAIN, PARALYSIS, DIFFICULT FRIENDSHIPS

THE SHORT STORY—When Teresa's mother died at a young age, Teresa's father sent her away to be educated at a convent. He thought Teresa had become too rebellious, because she was very interested in boys, socializing, and fashion. However, in Teresa's monastery, the sisters would have visitors who included flirtatious young men, wealthy society members, and other people who would engage in small talk and unnecessary drama. Though these things interrupted Teresa's prayer life, which was developing steadily after a period of serious illness, it was hard for her to distance herself from them. Teresa's participation ended abruptly, however, when she had a serious seizure. The suffering and losses caused by her ongoing seizures made her turn away from prayer at first, but several years later, Teresa was able to dive so deep into her prayer life that she experienced many visions and even physical sensations. For this experience she was often made fun of and mocked, even humiliated by those in positions of leadership. This did not break her spirit. Instead, it gave Teresa the fuel to begin her own convent, and she rewrote the Rule to emphasize simplicity. Members would give up their property, stop wearing shoes, work for their living, and prioritize forgiveness and joy. The order became known as the Discalced Carmelites. On this mission of reform, Teresa courageously braved not only the elements of dangerous journeys but also the religious authorities who continued to condemn her works.

BY MADISON CHASTAIN

I hate Bernini's sculpture *The Ecstasy of St. Teresa*. There she is, collapsed; her eyes rolled back, mouth open, an angel atop her, piercing her with an arrow. The innuendo is plain, and is suggested by Teresa's own writings, for God was indeed her spouse. I understand the mastery of the piece, folding stone into fabric and clouds, but the invasiveness makes my skin crawl. After she died, Teresa's body was literally ripped limb from limb by her own friends and the faithful, who ignored Church protocol to respect the dead just so they could keep pieces of her for themselves.

This is a woman often depicted as out of control of her own body. We understand now, through advancements in medical science and analysis of her writings, that Teresa probably experienced epileptic seizures.

Calling her ecstasies "epileptic" does not reduce their miracle, however. She experienced profound truths in the midst of them that enliven the Carmelite order and embolden the faithful who read her writings to this day.

But she was chronically ill; that much is clear from her biography. Her ability to offer her body to God, that He might unite Himself to her amid unimaginable discomfort, astounds me as a chronically ill person myself.

But she was *not* offering her body over to *us*. This is crucial. Teresa of Avila spent her young adult life fighting against her love of romance, worldly luxuries, and her body. The result of her efforts was a redirection of her "wickedness" to its proper owner: God. The pleasure she was blessed by God to have experienced, if truly akin to sexual intimacy, as most interpretations claim, shouldn't be plastered on every piece of her writing. I wouldn't want to be known by what I look like mid-coitus. That's not the author picture I would choose.

And while I'm all for celebrating the relationship between woman's sexuality and God, if we avoid identifying Teresa as chronically ill, we're still looking not at her whole body but at severed pieces.

I don't think Teresa's ecstasies alone were what destined her for sainthood. Teresa is everywoman's saint. She never left home without a book. She loved her family, socializing, clothes, and perfume. She held her confessors accountable when they knew less theology than she did. She was a type-A hostess who did everything to the extreme to impress others (and then felt guilty about it, too).

I met her years after she met me. Having forgotten that I needed to pick one, flipping through the book of saint names the week before my eighth-grade Confirmation, I noticed there were three Teresas: St. Teresa of Avila, St. Thérèse of Lisieux, and (then) Blessed Teresa of Calcutta. I figured one of them was bound to be good, so I slapped "Teresa" on my name tag and thought nothing else of it.

Then, as a freshman in college, I took a class on the saints. Br. Michael Meister, FSC, regaled us with tales of Teresa's life, emphasizing her wit, particularly the story of a trip that ended with Teresa drenched after a storm upturned her carriage. She joked with God later in her journal, "If this is how you treat your friends, it's no wonder you have so few of them!" She was a nun, a mystic, the first female Doctor of the Church. She was committed to St. Joseph, and she struggled to combat reluctance and waywardness for the sake of trust in God. Most important to me? She was a writer of humor, anger, and faith.

I knew immediately she was the saint for me. After that class I handed myself over to her intercessory friendship. She herself knew the importance of good, true friendships and wrote often about the difficulty of finding them.

That's who I see in this modern icon: Teresa, my friend. Laughing at whatever joke I just told, grasping my hand with sympathy as I describe my chronic illness symptoms, and reminding me to write to God about it all. This is St. Teresa of Avila, social butterfly with a contemplative habit, inviting us in. No invasive taking required.

I know she continues to freely give of herself through her intercession on my behalf. At the end of college, I was off to Tulsa for a year of volunteer teaching, and the guy I was falling for was off to Canada for graduate school. We went our separate ways, thinking we couldn't manage a long-distance relationship. After three months of daily texting and video chatting, I stuffed all the courage I had in a bag and flew to Canada to assert that we were *already doing* long distance. On October 15, Teresa of Avila's feast day, I landed in Edmonton and my long-distance guy and I had our first real date. Five years later we were married with a relic of St. Teresa of Avila herself overlooking us from the altar.

PRAYER

Lord Jesus,

Inspired by the life and writings of St. Teresa of Avila,
Be our friend.
Aid us in prayer.
Decrease our restlessness.
Help us to hear your truth in the midst of bodily affliction.
Unite us to Yourself to increase our joy.
"If you do not want [us] so busy, deliver [us] from it."
Give us "courage for whatever comes in life."
And "from silly devotions and sour-faced saints, deliver us"
Turning instead our attention to Your righteous fury at injustice, and the needs of Your people.
That we may be Your body, Your hands, Your eyes, and Your feet.

Through the intercession of Your most loving earthly father St. Joseph, to whom St. Teresa had a most earnest devotion.
And through the intercession of St. Teresa of Avila herself, who beckons us into holy friendship and inspires us to share our lives with others in word and action.
We ask these things—and entrust the silent intentions of our hearts—to your most Holy Name.
Amen.

MADISON CHASTAIN is a Chicago-based California native who writes about the body, chronic illness, disability, interreligious relationships, faith, and culture. She works in Catholic higher education in marketing and communications, and is a proud Special Religious Education and Development (SPRED) catechist and L'Arche Chicago volunteer. She has written for *The Young Catholic Woman, FemCatholic, The Catholic Woman, Live Today Well Co.,* and the *American Catholic Studies* journal. She is currently working on two book projects, one with *LifeTeen* and another with *Live Today Well Co.* You can find more of her work at theologyforeverybody.com and on Instagram @maddsienicole.

T'S STATEMENT—Brigid's sense of humor is displayed in her expression—a bold, ous smile. Her earrings are the St. Brigid's cross (in metalwork, which she estab- a school for), and her cow print shirt is a symbol of the cow that came to feed her infancy, as well as her patronage of livestock. She also has a tattoo of flames to lize the eternal flame she and her first cosisters tended in the convent. Her green epresents the miracle in which her cape grew endlessly when she asked for land onvent and was given only as much as her cape could cover.

BORN: **~451**

DIED: **~525**

FEAST: **FEBRUARY 1**

PATRON OF BLACKSMITHS, LIVESTOCK, CHILDREN OF ABUSIVE PARENTS, DAIRIES, BABIES, POETS, MIDWIVES, IRELAND

THE SHORT STORY—Brigid's historicity is often debated because, according to legend, St. Brigid's origin is in the Celtic goddess Brigid. She was born in Ireland to a Christian mother who was enslaved in the court of her father, Dubhthach, the chieftain. Dubhthach's wife forced him to sell Brigid and her mother to a druid. But according to some accounts, when the druid tried to feed her, Brigid would vomit, so instead a cow would appear to sustain her. When she turned ten, she was sent back to her father as a servant. He was so frustrated with her charity, though, that he tried to sell her to the king. Several times her father attempted to arrange a marriage for her, but Brigid had no interest. Instead, she founded a monastery with other women in Kildare. She also founded an art school focusing on metalwork and illumination. Brigid was said to have performed many miracles before her death, including restoring the sight of a blind nun, changing water into beer for a leper colony, controlling the weather, giving two girls the ability to speak, and blinding a man who mocked her.

BY KERRY CAMPBELL

As a daughter of parents born and raised in South Boston in the 1950s and '60s, I am no stranger to St. Brigid of Kildare. My family took our Irish heritage seriously, and we celebrated St. Patrick's Day each year with pride. My three sisters and I all bear Irish names: Shauna, Kerry, Erin, and Molly.

The holiday, fun as it was, was no deep dive into our Irish culture. We wore the green, sang the songs, ate the corned beef and cabbage, and cheered Sts. Patrick and Brigid without knowing much at all about who they actually were. Without understanding, an icon can become a caricature, especially when a hero or a saint is tied to a flag or a holiday, as Brigid certainly is here in America.

It was years before I realized that the simple cross above my front door, a gift from my Irish mother, was a St. Brigid cross. In all honesty, I don't remember her giving it to me or the ceremony of it, but it was so like her to provide my sisters and me with touchstones of our history. Each of us has a collection of Irish Belleek pottery, one piece given to us every year at Christmastime, and I'll just speak for myself: I never appreciated the gift at the time. Now that my mother is in Heaven, I look at these pieces and to the past with a more earnest and open lens. In the same way, as we look back and rediscover the story of a saint, we can find the lessons they were teaching all along as we remember their humanity and relate it to our own.

Brigid was a trailblazer, a leader in a time and at a place where the leadership of a woman would have been scoffed at. She broke from the wishes of her powerful father and entered a convent, later starting monasteries for both nuns and monks, and even opening a school of art. But it's the story of the weaving of the St. Brigid cross that captures my attention and connects me to her even now.

As the story goes, a pagan chieftain lay dying. Troubled in body and spirit, his family sent for Brigid to bring him some sense of calm and forbearance. As she sat with the man, she picked up rushes from the floor and began weaving a cross while telling the story of Jesus's life, death, and resurrection. Peace came to the chieftain as Brigid spoke, and as the story goes, he was baptized in Christ just before his death.

It wasn't uncommon to find rushes or straw scattered on a floor in the time Brigid lived. They provided insulation and kept an earthen floor tidy, but it was Brigid's creative use of what was at hand that can give us encouragement and direction today. To that point in time, Brigid had done great and unexpected things, things for which she was known—which elevated her name and caused the family to call her to the dying chieftain's side. But in the moment, while seated next to a dying man, Brigid used the power of the Gospel, of encounter, and of what was readily available to bring new light to one human life. We can do the same.

Sometimes we can get so caught up in our purpose, our vocation, or our legacy that we forget our ultimate story will be seen through the lens of our encounters and our connections with other humans. We can hope the ones who survive us will tell how we used the resources we had at hand to leave this world a little better than we found it. Brigid teaches us to pay attention to the leading of the Spirit in things great and small, and to let Him work through us to write our stories. As we look around us at what's at hand today—our time, talents, experiences, and material possessions—we can ask for the leading of St. Brigid to help us determine how to use our resources well for the furthering of the Kingdom, one encounter at a time.

PRAYER

St. Brigid, your feast day marks the beginning of spring in Ireland. Help us to embrace your example in this springtime of our faith lives, opening ourselves up to the possibilities for the best use of our time, talent, imagination, and material goods to bring the light of the Gospel to God's beloved people. Help us to participate with the Holy Spirit in small and big ways, right where we find ourselves today with what we have at hand. We pray in the name of Jesus. Amen.

KERRY CAMPBELL is a writer, podcaster, preschool music teacher, music minister, and mom to two grown kids. Kerry's weekly podcast series, *Raised Catholic,* aims at making a space where all cradle Catholics feel welcome, wherever they are on their faith journey. Find Kerry's writing on her blog at kerrycampbell.org and on Instagram @kerrycampbellwrites, and please say hello!

OUR LADY UN-DOER OF KNOTS

FEAST: **SEPTEMBER 27**

MARIAN DEVOTION

THE SHORT STORY—As early as the late second century, St. Irenaeus wrote in his book *Against Heresies,* "The knot of Eve's disobedience was loosed by the obedience of Mary. For what the virgin Eve had bound fast through unbelief, this did the virgin Mary set free through faith." But the particular devotion was not made popular until the early 1600s, when a German couple, Sophie and Wolfgang Langenmantel, were on the brink of divorce until they sought counsel from a local priest. They prayed to St. Mary to be able to save their relationship, and Wolfgang brought the couple's wedding ribbon (which had been used to tie the two together symbolically during the ceremony) on his visit to the priest. While praying, the priest lifted the ribbon to an image of Mary and asked her to "untie the knots" of Wolfgang's marriage. The ribbon miraculously brightened and untangled itself, and the couple reconciled afterward. A painting of Mary untying knots was commissioned by Sophie and Wolfgang's grandson, who became a priest. Recently, Pope Francis has made this Marian devotion popular again, not just for marital problems but for all anxieties, worries, and unsolvable issues.

ARTIST'S STATEMENT—Mary, as someone who was married to a regular person like so many of us, does understand the problems in our relationships and in our lives. I wanted her to look like she knows how we feel when we just can't figure something out or how to fix it. Her nails assist her in her work, and her hair mimics the thread, made completely of purposeful "knots."

BY MARIE HEIMANN

On a cold, rainy Holy Thursday night sitting in the car beside my boyfriend outside the adoration chapel, I was anxiously awaiting a conversation that would determine the next chapter of my life. We were at the end of a nine-day novena to Our Lady Undoer of Knots, and I could not wait to tell my boyfriend I wanted to spend the rest of my life with him. The plan was to share our decision after we prayed, but I couldn't wait a minute longer and so I asked him what he had decided. Nothing could have prepared me for what happened next.

We had been dating for a couple years before this moment, so marriage was constantly brought up. He liked to take his time with decisions. I was the opposite and decided things pretty quickly. I was anxious because I wanted to tell him how resolved I was to marry him, and how excited I was to be his wife. Unfortunately, he had come to a different conclusion.

He told me I had been treating him hurtfully and tore him down, and that he didn't know how he could continue allowing someone to treat him that way. He broke up with me. I was utterly devastated. In shock I got out of the car, began crying the heaviest tears, and wandered around downtown in the dark and the rain. My now ex-boyfriend found me and asked if he could drive me home. I agreed. That night was one of the hardest of my life. I had thought I was going to spend the rest of my life with this man. I was wrong.

The following morning, Good Friday, we both went to the church to pray, each not knowing the other was going. We sat together, and while I was praying beside him I became aware that I did have some deeply rooted issues that were causing me to treat him poorly. I realized I didn't have to continue with my behavior toward him and there was still hope. I asked Our Lady Undoer of Knots to work out this one last knot, which could change our lives forever. I knew it would be a long journey, but I was ready to learn and grow. I followed a sudden urge to put my hand on his and ask him to come over for breakfast to talk things through. He agreed, reluctantly.

We spent the next four hours cooking together, eating, and talking about everything that had led to that moment. We were both humbled and ready to heal. It was as if the horribly tangled knot was being unraveled before our eyes. He decided he would spend the weekend with his family for Easter and would return with his decision.

I am overjoyed and humbled to share that that man is now my husband of ten years and we have the most beautiful four boys, two daughters in Heaven, and another boy due very soon. The story of the early years of our relationship, with its constant knots—which I dreaded sharing with our kids someday—is now one of my favorite stories to share. Mary Undoer of Knots has appeared throughout my messy, mundane life. She gathered up all of my knots, just as she still does today, and lovingly and unexpectedly began to undo them.

Of course, prayer does not always produce miracles, but asking Mary to untangle the knots that creep up in our lives can give us the fortitude, patience, peace, clarity, and strength to endure and resolve them as they come. It can also have a positive impact on our mental health, knowing we are not alone, we have an advocate, and she loves us as only a mother can.

Racism, the degradation of human life, sexism, war, and so much more plague our world with unrest and tension. As I reflect on this image of Our Lady Undoer of Knots, I'm reminded again how intricately Mary sees us, not just the big scary things in the world, but the messy mundane things stirring up in our hearts. The things we are tempted to diminish because of the vast problems of the world are the very things Mary wants to bring into her fold and work out for and with us.

Oftentimes figurative knots in our lives can manifest as actual knots in our bodies and nervous systems. I have struggled with anxiety all of my adult life, but Mary is constantly reminding me that when I feel anxious, she wants me to return to her, ask for her help, trust in her motherly care, and take my knots so she can guide me through undoing them, one by one.

Our Lady Undoer of Knots desires for all of us to bring our knots to her, the great and the small ones. Your pain matters to your Heavenly Mother.

PRAYER

Mary, please help us to relinquish our knots to you,
so you may gather them up and undo them one by one.
Help us to surrender every day, every moment,
to your motherly care. Amen.

MARIE HEIMANN lives in Fort Wayne, Indiana, with her five boys and her husband, Cory. She loves to draw and letter meaningful and encouraging quotes from the saints and Scripture, and nuggets of truth she learns in therapy. She owns a home decor and home goods shop, Fawnly, where she sells all her original art.

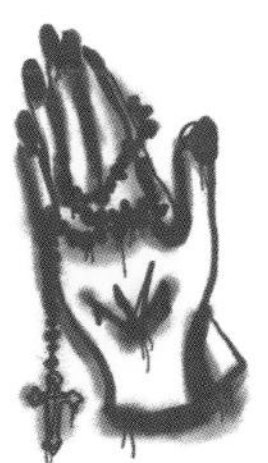

STS. PRISCILLA AND AQUILA

ARTIST'S STATEMENT—Both Priscilla and Aquila wear camping gear in this image (with Aquila's vest even bearing a tent symbol) as a nod to the pair's work as tentmakers and travelers. They hold each other and look to each other to symbolize their equality, with Priscilla supporting Aquila, a posture opposite from what is normally seen in posed images of heterosexual couples.

BORN: **FIRST CENTURY**
DIED: **LATE FIRST CENTURY**
FEAST: **JULY 8**
PATRONS OF LOVE, MARRIAGE, PARTNERSHIP

THE SHORT STORY—Priscilla and her husband, Aquila, happened to meet St. Paul while in Corinth, where they had fled when Emperor Claudius ordered Jewish families to leave the city of Rome. While there St. Paul lived and worked with the two of them, since their trade, like his, was tentmaking. As he worked alongside them, he taught them about Christianity, and soon they became his most well-versed companions. Priscilla and Aquila were dedicated friends of Paul, helping him found churches and preach. Some also wonder whether Priscilla was the author of the anonymous Letter to the Hebrews. This is debated because of the letter's uncommon anonymity, which may have been necessary given the likelihood that the audience would have rejected it if the author was discovered to be female. In addition, throughout the New Testament, Priscilla's name is mentioned with her husband's, and usually before it, indicating that she was an important early Church leader, or held the role of a presbyter. Whether Priscilla and Aquila were martyred or died naturally is unknown, but it is most likely they were killed in Rome around the same time as Paul.

BY INDIA JADE MCCUE

I remember standing in the doorway and trying to slow my breath. I could hardly contain my excitement. We had just moved into our new home. And while boxes were everywhere and a clogged pipe caused a small flood under our feet, the palpable joy of owning a blank space was truly overwhelming in the best way.

But this wasn't just any space. It was the second home we had purchased within one year, and the third place we'd moved to in just a few short months of being married. I felt like a nomad, having everything that resembled familiarity swept from underneath me. Yet as we stood in this new place, something felt different. There was a peace throughout the space.

When I was a young girl who dreamt of one day being married, there was a lot of talk about what it meant to be a future wife—uh, I mean woman. Well-meaning folks would often discuss a woman's virtuous nature. Things like becoming a mother, abstaining from crass language, and dressing modestly (whatever that means) were often brought up. But unfortunately, there was not a lot of discussion around becoming a Godly teammate. Having been married for some time now, I can say that having and being a solid, Godly teammate means so much more for my marriage than the length of my shorts ever will.

In the New Testament, the Apostle Paul briefly mentions an inspirational couple who, according to Paul in the Letter to the Romans, "risked their lives" for him, and for the early Church (Romans 16:3–5 NIV). Priscilla and Aquila, a Jewish couple, exemplify the team-based marriage I strive after today.

The power couple were tentmakers by trade. They worked jointly with their hands. It is highly likely there were many years when they hammered and sewed away, gently assembling structures that others would use for shelter and gathering. Together in their vocation, they built homes for God's children to abide in.

When racial injustice forced them out of their own home, they retreated to Greece, where they met the Apostle Paul. What probably looked like the worst situation to be in (losing their home, fleeing for their lives, and being forced to start over) led to their legacy living on through Scripture. Paul mentions that Priscilla and Aquila were the hosts of the local church meetings (not unlike present day small groups, I imagine—minus the Lacroix and Lovesac furniture).

This tells us that these tentmakers who built homes for others now were the ones opening their own home (tent) for anyone in need of physical or spiritual shelter.

I've moved more times than I can count. Whether for jobs, schools, a pandemic, or marriage, the concept of home has become muddled for me in the wake of early adulthood. As I've explored what it means to be a wife and what a God-honoring home can look like, I am grateful for the example of Priscilla and Aquila. Nothing compares to working alongside my husband as a teammate. We take on many projects, and the experience of ministering, laboring, and creating with the one I share my life with is a true blessing. Priscilla and Aquila realized the impact their actions could have for the Gospel was simply greater when done together than if done apart. Even in the face of nomadic uncertainty, they would put down roots again somewhere new, and start once more.

Furthermore, the space they inhabited was not limited to comfort for themselves only but rather opened up for others. I often think we devalue the ministry of home. We mindlessly rush through meals in front of screens, compare the square footage we have with others we know nothing about, and converse less in order to work more. When in fact, the ministry that can happen under a roof is all a part of God's Kingdom building. Priscilla and Aquila knew that, having built homes for others, they could extend hospitality through cultivating a space full of the peace of Heaven right where they were.

Looking around my physical home, I can't help but smile. My teammate is with me, and though the work before us is vast (and the amount of YouTubing home projects is, too) the potential of our space is under God's blessing and in our hands. This will be the home we will cry in, laugh in, and grow our family in. Dreams will take flight from here, and people, lost and found, will always be welcome.

PRAYER

May the Kingdom grow as we open our homes (tents) and extend what we have for the Lord's glory and our neighbors' good.

INDIA JADE MCCUE is a multipassionate creative entrepreneur, wedding photographer, and award-winning actress. She earned her BFA in Advertising and Graphic Design from Columbus College of Art and Design in 2019 and has yet to stop creating since. Though travel is in her blood, India and her beloved husband, Ian, share a home with their two cats in Columbus, Ohio.

ST. CYPRIAN

BORN: **~200**

DIED: **258**

FEAST: **SEPTEMBER 16**

PATRON OF NORTH AFRICA, SECOND CHANCES, LEADERS

THE SHORT STORY—Cyprian was born into a polytheistic faith in northern Africa. He was a great speaker and lawyer, but when he discovered Christianity, he dove all the way in, becoming bishop only two years after converting and giving away all he owned. During a Roman persecution, he fled and hid so that his parish could still have a leader through his letters. When he returned to his community, he advocated for forgiveness for those who had abandoned their faith in fear. Soon after, his leadership was tested when his followers were attacked and many of them were enslaved, a drought and famine befell the area, and a plague broke out. Cyprian led by being present among his people, personally caring for and attending to them, calling out Church leaders and even the Pope who did not assist the hurting. Despite his courageous benevolence, he was martyred when he refused to sacrifice to Roman gods. He was known as being cheerful, well respected, and greatly loved, often righteously angry over injustice.

ARTIST'S STATEMENT—I wanted St. Cyprian, with a steady and assured expression, to be a commanding figure while also seeming approachable, expressing his personality in his hair and T-shirt. Because he was devoted to his community for his whole life, while also seemingly a gentle soul with a darker past, I wanted him to look like someone who would give a great hug and at the same time tell off the religious authorities who were selfish and causing pain.

What a grandeur of spirit it is to struggle with all the powers of an unshaken mind against so many onsets of devastation and death! What sublimity, to stand erect amid the desolation of the human race, and not to lie prostrate with those who have no hope in God; but rather to rejoice, and to embrace the benefit of the occasion; that in thus bravely showing forth our faith, and by suffering endured, going forward to Christ by the narrow way that Christ trod, we may receive the reward of His life and faith according to His own judgment!

—ST. CYPRIAN[6]

BY MARCIE ALVIS WALKER

The problem with second chances is all the broken bones, the scarred skin, the dried pus and putrid excuses you have to tend to in order to get to them. Second chances always look better in retrospect. The before picture of anyone in need of another chance is nothing any of us want to see. But the after? Wow. Magnificent! Miraculous.

I feel a little sorry for St. Cyprian. It must be awfully hard to be a patron saint of second chances. The crashes and burns he must watch. The relapses and setbacks. The flare-ups of degradation and disgrace he has no choice but to see. The spiraling litany of pathetic excuses and all the justifications of all the broken promises he must suffer before the witness of the light of mercy and renewal.

These days I wonder if the widespread and rising contagion of so many desperate prayers to be forgiven, to be uncanceled, to be allowed back at the table, feels as devastating as the persecution and plague St. Cyprian endured in his lifetime. But of course, being on the other side of ultimate redemption, he's only braver, with an even greater "grandeur of spirit" and "unshaken mind."

Right now, for everyone in this country, I so want a grandeur of spirit and an unshaken mind. After these past few years, more than my own peace and solitude, I want the rested assurance of an unshaken mind against so many onslaughts of devastation and death! I ache for the kind of brave dignity it would take for people to stand united as we look back on the desolate stories of history. I yearn to stand firm in the midst of the sorrow, not giving in to those who are so scared of our truth that it renders them hopeless to solve its lingering problems. I wish for nothing more than a second chance for our country. So, I too must join in the cacophonous lament that sometimes feels like it will end me.

And maybe that's the point of weeping after all—to use the tears to wipe the slate clean so we can begin again.

Though the powers that be refuse to hear us, St. Cyprian listens, endures, and intercedes, reminding us that our suffering is the way to go forward, though the Shepherd's gate is so narrow. *Go forward,* he says. *Beyond the gate waits a pasture green with second beginnings.*

PRAYER

St. Cyprian—
Refusing to divert, right or left,
You stood by your convictions in the center
cradling your heart in the hand of Jesus.
Refusing to sink into despair,
You embraced joy in the face of plague and persecution
hiding your body beneath the wing of the Spirit.
Refusing to marginalize
You opened yourself to the unforgiven
uniting your humanity in the radiance of God.
Center and cradle the disunited.
Hide and embrace the plagued and the persecuted.
Open and unite the marginalized and unforgiven.
May our hearts ever be in the hand of Jesus.
May our bodies ever be beneath the wing of the Spirit.
May our humanity ever be the radiance of God.
Amen.

MARCIE ALVIS WALKER is the creator of the popular Instagram feed *Black Coffee with White Friends*. She is also the creator of *Black Eyed Stories*. Marcie is passionate about what it means to embrace intersectionality, diversity, and inclusion in our spiritual lives. She lives in Chicago with her husband; her college-age kid, Max; and their dog, Evie. Her book, *Everybody Come Alive: A Memoir in Essays,* debuts in the spring of 2023.

ST. IGNATIUS OF LOYOLA

RTIST'S STATEMENT—In this icon Ignatius—possibly still a little cocky, but focused nd dedicated due to his competitive nature—studies and writes even while imprisoned. othing at all could stop this man, despite the incredible number of times he was reatened or was physically, intellectually, or theologically pushed back.

BORN: **OCTOBER 23, 1491**

DIED: **JULY 31, 1556**

FEAST: **JULY 31**

PATRON OF THE JESUITS, SOLDIERS, EDUCATORS AND STUDENTS, RETREATS

THE SHORT STORY—Ignatius was sent to work in the Spanish court, where he fell in love with a materialistic lifestyle. When he was eighteen Ignatius joined the military. His life took a turn, however, when a cannonball shattered his leg in battle. While recovering, he read books. There weren't many options, so he was forced to read about Christianity and the lives of the saints, resulting in a conversion of his heart. Once he had recovered he lived in the Spanish countryside for about a year, begging for food to get by, working at a hospital, and praying for hours a day. He also spent much time in a cave, reflecting and meditating, and it was there he decided he would become a priest. To do this he had to enter school with children and begin his studies at the most basic level. He spent the next eleven years learning in schools across Europe. While studying in Paris, Ignatius was roommates with two men, Francis Xavier and Peter Faber. These three together formed what is now called the Society of Jesus. In 1540 the Pope made the order official, and Ignatius was elected the leader.

BY FR. JAMES MARTIN

I've always felt somewhat guilty that I don't feel as warmly toward St. Ignatius Loyola, the founder of the Society of Jesus (a.k.a. the Jesuits), as I think I should. Over the years I've heard a few other Jesuits (very quietly) confess the same thing. Unlike women and men such as St. Thérèse of Lisieux, St. John XXIII, or St. Bernadette

Soubirous (three of my favorite saints), St. Ignatius generally doesn't evoke affection among Catholics.

Some of that has to do with the man's character—which, while generous and warm, was also quite austere. Perhaps some of that is because he spent many years as an administrator: superior general of the Society of Jesus. That meant some necessary toughness when it came to dealing with a few recalcitrant Jesuits around the world trying to figure out what their religious order was.

But to see Ignatius as a hard man is to misunderstand him. The man born Iñigo de Loyola in the Basque country of Spain in 1491 was given to weeping in prayer, so moved was he by God's loving presence. He patiently served as a spiritual director and counselor to men and women from all walks of life. He would dance Basque "jigs" to cheer up disconsolate Jesuits in Rome.

And he was humble enough to return to school as an adult, going so far as to take classes with boys when he realized that his education was insufficient—which is what I like to think this image depicts.

Nor was Ignatius inflexible. He was constantly changing his plans when things didn't work out—even after long periods of prayer, discernment, and decision making. When he was a young man he thought he was going to be a great soldier, but the cannonball that shattered his leg ended his military career forever. Later he thought that he should live like an ascetic, but he found that the practices he had embraced harmed his health and he had to start eating better. He thought he would move to the Holy Land, but he was turned away by the Franciscans who were organizing the possibility, probably because he seemed a little crazy.

At each juncture, Ignatius had to discern what to do when it seemed like his path was blocked. As a result, he is sometimes called the "Patron Saint of Plan B." Ignatius shows us that the path to holiness can sometimes be confusing and rather circuitous. So don't worry too much about changing your mind or your course. Ignatius and many others did it before you did—and reached their destination all the same.

Maybe a better way of describing my feelings toward Ignatius is to say that I'm grateful for his great gift to the world. And despite what many graduates of Jesuit middle schools, high schools, and colleges might say, his greatest gift was not the vast network of schools that spans the globe today, but something simpler. Something that changed my own life. Ignatius's greatest gift was the spirituality he left behind, a spirituality that can be (accurately) summed up as "finding God in all things."

What does this mean? Simply put—and here you get a sense of Ignatius's flexibility—God can be found in any person, circumstance, or situation. God is not confined to experiences that one has in church, or by reading the Bible, as important as those things are. God can be found everywhere and in every person. That insight liberated me as a young man. And still does today.

But there's more. Ignatian spirituality says that every person can encounter God in their own lives, no matter who they are. God wants a relationship with each of us, and God reaches out to start and nourish that relationship. All we have to do is notice where God is active in our daily lives and in our prayer.

That simple idea was so controversial in Ignatius's time that it got him jailed. It's controversial in our time, too—when some people want to deny the activity of God in our individual consciences. But as Ignatius said, "The Creator can deal directly with the creature." For all this, I'm grateful. And, truth be told, I do have affection for you, after all. Thank you, Ignatius.

PRAYER

St. Ignatius, we ask you for your prayers today:
That we may not freak out when things don't go our way.
Because it didn't bother you when you had to change your plans.
You knew that God was with you, no matter what happened.
Help us always want to do God's will,
Even if we can't quite figure it out yet.
Help us to notice God in things both big and small.
And help us find the wisdom and discernment that enabled you

To lead such a bold, fruitful, and holy life,
In our own way and in our own time,
Through Christ Our Lord.
Amen.

JAMES MARTIN, S.J., is a Jesuit priest, editor at large of *America* magazine, consultor to the Vatican's Dicastery for Communication, and author of many books, including the *New York Times* bestsellers *The Jesuit Guide, Jesus: A Pilgrimage,* and most recently, *Learning to Pray.*

STS. PERPETUA AND FELICITY

ARTIST'S STATEMENT—These portraits, designed to go together in a two-piece frame, are meant to fit together in other ways as well. One, in using similar colors that I found to be symbolic of their intimate, fiery, and courageous energy. Another, in their mug-shot-like poses. Felicity's position as an enslaved person is evident in her jewelry that's like chains, while Perpetua's hair is somewhat loose and representative of the story of her fixing it. They both wear plain T-shirts and have expressions as determined as they are saddened to leave their loved ones behind.

BORN: **~181**

DIED: **203**

FEAST: **MARCH 7**

PATRON OF MOTHERS, EXPECTANT MOTHERS, RANCHERS AND BUTCHERS, BEST FRIENDS, WOMEN'S RELATIONSHIPS, PRISONERS, CARTHAGE, AND CATALONIA

THE SHORT STORY—Perpetua was a noblewoman in northern Africa in the late second century, and Felicity was her close friend and enslaved servant. Both were studying Christianity when Emperor Severus announced that all people must sacrifice to the Roman gods or be put to death. Felicity, Perpetua, and a few other Christians were rounded up and imprisoned, despite Felicity being eight months pregnant and Perpetua having a young son of her own. Perpetua had a dream of her imminent martyrdom, and of a ladder to Heaven. It was against the law for pregnant women to be killed, but Felicity wanted to die with Perpetua instead of with strangers in the next round of executions. Her prayers were answered when her baby was born only three days before the games in which they had been condemned to die. On the day of the games, while the men were attacked by wild animals, Felicity and Perpetua clung to each other. After a wild cow charged and severely wounded Perpetua, she took a moment to fix her hair and then both women held on to each other until the end, when the gladiators entered the arena and swiftly beheaded them.

BY SARA BILLUPS

Though I have never set foot in Tunisia, I do know something about fostering life in the midst of uncertainty, alongside friends, in order to bear witness to strength in the midst of trials. Be they pandemic, global persecution, or personal affliction.

A neighbor walked by my house the other day holding her newborn baby in a sling. Her shoulders were weighted and weary. "How are you?" I asked. She was just back to work at a local hospital, and she had to pump her milk in a small, designated nursing mother's closet. As I recalled a similar season in my life a decade prior, we talked together about the loud mechanical repetition of the breast pump and the work of carrying an insulated freezer bag from pumping closet to home. The full and wide weight of carrying a new thing.

We are weary, mothers in our present time. Some of us move into parenting with the gift of bearing weariness in safety. We read about growing a child from a poppy seed to a blueberry to a mini watermelon on websites for expectant mothers. We birth babies in a wave of blood and water. Then we clean and heal. In safety, this process is magic: a revelation, through which we are shepherded by midwives and medical professionals.

But not all women are able to grow poppy seeds or blueberries. Some babies are born breathing, and some are not. Some mothers are sick while nursing, some children have cells divide and multiply and are living until they are not. Sometimes the body of a child grows strong but her mind twists and breaks into sadness or worry. We bear the beauty and the brokenness, and so do our children.

I thought the vulnerability of pregnancy would end and the present work of mothering would begin after my children were born. But I learned that vulnerability does not alleviate our tender and raw worry. Instead, vulnerability in lacking control shifts and morphs as a child grows from newborn to preschooler to gangly teen. Having experienced this makes me all the more grateful for the courage of Perpetua and Felicity.

Describing her separation from her young son in prison, Perpetua wrote in her diary, "I was tormented with anxiety for my baby . . . Such anxieties I suffered for many days." When her son joined her in prison, she wrote, "I at once recovered my health, and my prison became a palace to me and I would rather have been there than anywhere else."[7]

Perpetua and Felicity carried a faithfulness in relationship while facing oppression, imprisonment, and violent death. The friendship strengthened each woman. It was a visceral thing, this bond between two compassionate and fierce women. Completely loyal to God and each other, these bold and strong believers in the way of Jesus were also buoyed by their children.

Spiritual friendship—a relationship with the kind of friend who mothers you as you yourself mother—is a really rare thing. I've known it only once in my life. A few years ago I sat in a windowed nook in Hudson, New York, with this friend as she nursed her fifth child. We talked in the morning with a lot of longing for the Church and how God can change hardened hearts. We put the baby down to sleep at night and prayed in the window seat. At one point there was so much crying, we began laughing.

I would like to think we could all be as loving and loyal in true friendship as Perpetua and Felicity. I would like to think we could each mother living things, be they babies or creative projects or Church communities.

Pregnant Mary spent three months with pregnant Elizabeth, and their babies knew it. Jesus would be crucified and John would be beheaded, like Felicity and Perpetua, a much earlier kind of martyr. But no matter how near or far the separation between child and mother, there was a time of verdant growing in friendships before an ending. The limbs swimming in the stomach, twisting and sleeping, as the mothers grew close.

In our darkest moments, when fear presses us down and uncertainty hovers, sometimes all we can do is pray the word *help*. God often answers those prayers by sending other people to our aid; a friend, family member, or community may stand with us and allow us to say, like Perpetua, "I at once recovered my health."

I imagine the women surrounded in the arena, wild animals kicking dust, spectators watching from all directions. They stand in the presence of all their enemies and they face what's to come—

together. I imagine a shared look of recognition in the face of death when Perpetua and Felicity realize their story in Christ is just beginning. They left a message in a bottle, so to speak—a secret gift—as their children bore their names and their story would become a magnet drawing us all closer to courage.

PRAYER

> *Lord, as we grow new things that will one day have their own lives and uncertain futures, strengthen us to bear living love and a hope that is not dependent on our safety or a clear way forward. Be with us as we hold suffering in one hand and hope in the other.*

SARA BILLUPS is a Seattle-based writer. Her work has appeared in *The New York Times, Christianity Today, Ekstasis,* and *Bitter Scroll,* her monthly newsletter. Sara is completing her DM in the Sacred Art of Writing at the Peterson Center for the Christian Imagination at Western Theological Seminary. Her first book, *Orphaned Believers,* is forthcoming from Baker Books.

ARTIST'S STATEMENT—Using actual photos of Mary as some of my references, I wanted to convey in this icon her dignity, determination, and unwavering strength in the pursuit of what was necessary and right. She has eucalyptus and gum tree leaves, which are native to Australia, in her hair, and her tattoo is the symbol of her religious order.

BORN: **JANUARY 15, 1842**

DIED: **AUGUST 8, 1909**

FEAST: **AUGUST 8**

PATRON OF AUSTRALIA, SURVIVORS OF SEXUAL ASSAULT, WHISTLEBLOWERS

THE SHORT STORY—In Victoria, Australia, after working as a governess for two years, Mary accepted a teaching position and not long after, opened her own school. In 1866 Mary and her siblings joined the local priest, Fr. Woods, in founding a Catholic school in Penola. It was then that Mary, a sister, and several other women began to call themselves the Sisters of St. Joseph of the Sacred Heart. Mary's goal was to develop a school in South Australia specifically for rural children, and by 1871 that dream had come true with over 130 of her sisters teaching in forty schools. She also worked with children who were neglected or in danger, the elderly, the imprisoned, and the sick. Around this time Mary called out a local priest because of abuse, causing him to be sent back to Ireland. That priest's friend then convinced the bishop to sign an act that would have left the nuns homeless. When Mary would not retract her statement, he excommunicated her for disobeying him. While on his deathbed the bishop realized he had done wrong and reversed her excommunication. Mary's next mission, then, was to get formal approval for her order. She was declared official leader of the Sisters of St. Joseph of the Sacred Heart and remained steadfast in her decisions, which still made her unpopular among some peers. She continued her work until the day she died, providing more and better social services to people of all faiths in Australia than any other organization.

BY ISABEL MORBITZER

When I first knew I wanted to be a teacher, I thought the best part would be helping kids learn about the subjects I am passionate about and finding creative ways to make the material come alive for them. While I'm still excited about these things, I have learned over the past four years that the best part of teaching is the ability to help elevate the voice of each student. Education is a path to finding oneself and being able to discover passions. I have seen children who are in terrible positions: they might come from impoverished families, or be experiencing neglect, or be struggling with mental or physical ailments. Education raises their awareness and gives them respite from whatever hardships they must endure. It also allows them to grow as strong individuals that can stand up for what is right and speak out against injustice.

Mary MacKillop had an incredibly strong voice, and I think she knew how many more strong people she could influence by being an educator and starting her order. She also used her voice in the Church. She spoke about what was right, even if it went against the powerful Church leaders in her area.

As the patron saint of survivors of sexual assault, she's a source of hope because of how she used her voice. Sexual violence is all about power. To a survivor, it feels useless to try to fight the person who has already taken so much. Therefore, many do not speak up because they fear that they will be subjected to more violence, or that they will not be taken seriously. They carry the pain of the assault, which is tragically amplified when they are misunderstood or even victim-blamed.

I don't know how Mary was able to compromise her safety and entire life in order to stand up for herself and all others who might have been hurt. Her strength must have come from her belief that someone greater and something bigger was backing her up. I believe that strength comes from God, and it's what our faith should do. It should make us powerful. I feel stronger knowing that when my voice falters, I am not alone.

Mary, as the patron of whistleblowers, is a strong example of how we should stand against injustice today. She tried to make the situation within the Church better by exposing the problems she was seeing. She did not turn her back on the Church or try to "cancel" everyone within it. I have found it difficult to stay loyal to the Church because of multiple sexual abuse scandals, even within my own diocese. It is challenging for me to see so many problems and still find the strength to believe. It is hard for me to justify going to mass in the same church where someone had to face an atrocity. I have to both take inspiration from Mary and call out the problems I encounter but also continue to believe in God and the good we should all stand for, inside and outside the Church. Even after being kicked out of the Church, Mary still believed in God, and I want to do the same.

Like Mary, I am choosing to make education and helping others my priorities in life. I can use my voice to teach children how to treat one another with justice and respect. I can give them a voice in return, so if they ever face abuse, scandal, or hard times they can speak up when doing so is difficult. God will have their backs when things seem impossible, just as I know He has mine.

PRAYER

Inspire my voice, Lord. Help me to speak out for what is right and what is needed. Inspire my actions, so they can match the words I speak. Empower me even when I am broken down.

Thank you for having my back, and thank you for guiding my heart.

ISABEL MORBITZER attended Capital University and graduated with a degree in middle childhood education. She is passionate about creating a safe and rigorous learning environment for all students. She is from Columbus, Ohio, and spends her free time reading, baking, and playing with her cat.

ST. ÓSCAR ROMERO

ARTIST'S STATEMENT—The colors and flag of El Salvador, as well as the national bird (the torogoz), are featured prominently in this icon of St. Óscar Romero. Romero looks to this bird, a symbol of the country he loves and wants to save, with a wary but tender expression.

BORN: **AUGUST 15, 1917**

DIED: **MARCH 24, 1980**

FEAST: **MARCH 24**

PATRON OF EL SALVADOR, THE AMERICAS, THOSE WHO ARE PERSECUTED, RESISTANCE, SOCIAL JUSTICE

THE SHORT STORY—Óscar Romero was born and raised in El Salvador but completed his theology studies in Rome, where he was ordained, and he quickly became a popular, well-known priest. First ordained as a bishop, he later was made Archbishop of San Salvador. After he'd had only a few weeks in that role, however, Romero's good friend Jesuit priest Rutilio Grande was assassinated. As a result El Salvador's schools began to close and priests were removed from government negotiations and sent to be tortured and killed, along with many citizens who protested the leadership of the country. Romero could no longer stay silent. He began to speak out against the killings, the social injustice, and the deplorable poverty. In 1979 a paramilitary right-wing junta took control of El Salvador's government, and Romero criticized the United States for backing the group. He broadcast his sermons via radio in an effort to reach the people of El Salvador. In 1980 he was assassinated while he was celebrating mass by an unknown person likely affiliated with the government.

BY CAMERON BELLM

Put plainly, St. Óscar Romero gives me hope. Every time I am dismayed by how far this world is from the Kingdom of God and how rife it is with injustice, I remember him and his powerful prophetic example. I also take comfort in the fact that he wasn't always so bold and courageous. It took the assassination of a fellow priest to awaken him to the need to speak out against his country's violent government and terrible human rights abuses. Before his friend's assassination, Romero didn't want to get involved, didn't want to rock the boat. He was shy and bookish behind his big horn-rimmed glasses. Just like me. My faith was once something very myopic, something that really concerned only me. Óscar Romero helped widen my vision, leading me to see that my relationship with God is beautifully and necessarily intertwined in my relationships with other people.

When he could no longer refrain from speaking out against violence, corruption, and evil, Romero allowed himself to be utterly transformed by the fire of the Holy Spirit, even though he knew it would cost him his life. And it did. What I admire most in others is what I find most lacking in myself. I'm not a terribly courageous person. But Óscar Romero makes me believe that I can be. Every time I raise my voice against the violence of poverty, injustice, and oppression that plagues our country still, I imagine that I am but one singer in the chorus that carries on his work.

When he preached every Sunday, his voice ringing out through thousands of radios across the country, Romero always reminded his people that salvation history is being lived out all around us, in every place, at every time. He shone the light of the Gospel on El Salvador, illuminating the places where Christ was being crucified in the midst of present reality. And he also gave his people hope that the Resurrection, too, was all around them. The atrocities that Romero witnessed would be enough to shake anyone's faith, both in God and in humanity. But he held firm to the Gospel of Jesus Christ, constantly grieving the Passion, constantly rejoicing in the promise of the Resurrection.

When Óscar Romero chose to stand in solidarity with his oppressed people, he faced opposition from every corner, but most painfully from within the Church itself. Other priests and bishops denounced him as a communist and accused him of stirring up trouble and inciting violence. How very familiar those complaints sound, don't they, as we engage in justice work now, forty years later. What a beautiful reminder that we are in good and holy company.

Romero answered that the only violence he preached was the violence of love, the violence of the Crucifixion, which opened the door to redemption for us all. Amid constant denunciations and death threats, Óscar Romero stood firm. "We are not planting discord," he explained in a 1978 homily. "We are simply crying out to the God who is weeping."[8]

And doesn't God weep at the mess of the world in our day as well? What Óscar Romero understood was that a gospel that does not directly confront injustice and oppression is, in fact, no gospel at all. And when, week after week, he was accused of sullying God's holy Church with politics, Romero calmly explained, "The homily is not being 'political' when it points out political, social, and economic sins. It is simply the word of God becoming incarnate in our reality, which often reflects not God's reign but sin."[9] Today too there is plenty of resistance to the Church's involvement in social justice, against Her speaking plainly about the need to advocate for and with the most vulnerable and marginalized among us. How can we be silent about things that God cares about so deeply? Óscar Romero reminds us that we can't.

It would be impossible to overstate how very dangerous Óscar Romero's mission was, and he knew it. But he never stopped offering forgiveness to those who wanted him dead. In one of the last interviews he gave before he was murdered, he forgave and blessed his killers in advance and gave his people hope for the future, even a future without him. "A bishop will die," he said, "but the Church of God, which is the people, will never perish."[10]

As he came to understand that the end of his life was near, Romero stated, "I have frequently been threatened with death. I must say that, as a Christian, I do not believe in death without resurrection; if they kill me, I will rise again in the Salvadoran people."[11] Forty years later he has indeed risen again in countless Salvadorans who honor his memory and continue working for economic, social, and political justice. From his tiny country he has inspired people of faith, hope, and goodwill all over the world. I like to think that I too am among the many who carry his torch.

One of my favorite stories about Óscar Romero takes place during a Eucharistic procession in the city of Aguilares. As the people circled the main square, the National Guard stepped in and blocked the path, rifles pointing at the crowd. Everyone stopped and turned to Romero, who was at the back of the procession. He lifted the monstrance higher and called out, "¡Adelante!" ("Let us go forward!"). Little by little the people pushed forward until the National Guard retreated peacefully, lowering their guns.

I thought of this story several years ago as I marched in a pilgrimage from a parish in Tacoma to an immigration detention center, where many people seeking a better and safer life were being held indefinitely. When we arrived we held a bilingual mass outside the gates, the altar set up in the bed of a pickup truck. We sang and prayed in solidarity with our sisters and brothers locked inside and with several local organizations providing them legal counsel and material support. I marched in front, carrying our sign; it was the holiest ground my feet have ever walked upon. All these years later, Óscar Romero's voice still calls, to me and to all of us, "¡Adelante!"

PRAYER

St. Óscar Romero, ablaze with the love of God,
Light a fire in our hearts, too.
Lead us into the joyful and sorrowful work
Of solidarity with the suffering.
Let us never forget that the Kingdom of God
Is not an unattainable and far-off mirage,
But something we are called to build
With all our hands, with all our hearts,
Right here, right now.
Amen.

CAMERON BELLM is a Seattle-based writer and contemplative in action, combining her love of language with a deeply rooted spirituality to compose prayers, poems, essays, and devotionals linking our modern lives with our ancient faith. She is the author of *A Consoling Embrace: Prayers for a Time of Pandemic* and *No Unlikely Saints: A Mental Health Pilgrimage with Sacred Company.*

ST. JOHN

BORN: **6**

DIED: **100**

FEAST : **DECEMBER 27**

PATRON OF FRIENDSHIP, LOYALTY, LOVE, AUTHORS

THE SHORT STORY—John and his brother James were called by Jesus while they were out on their boat fishing, and both immediately left to follow him. Jesus called them "Sons of Thunder," possibly because of their quick tempers. John was present for all of Jesus's miracles described in the Gospels, even the Transfiguration, which only he, his brother, and St. Peter witnessed. John was known as "the disciple whom Jesus loved," and he was the only one of the twelve who did not run away when Jesus was crucified. John was present with Christ even at the cross. It was there that Jesus asked John to take care of Mary from then on. It is said that after Mary's Assumption, John preached about Jesus until he was banished by the Romans to the island of Patmos. He was sent there after he had survived numerous murder attempts, from being poisoned to being boiled alive. It was on Patmos that he is said to have written the Book of Revelation and later passed away, the only Apostle to die of natural causes.

ARTIST'S STATEMENT—I always imagined John out on his own, writing and smoking, after people tried to kill him so many times and all of his friends and fellow Apostles had been martyred. Because he is the patron of writers, an image of him that comes to mind for me is a traditional scholar with a pipe (though the cigarette is the modern version). I'm sure he wouldn't have been worried about lung cancer after all he had been through—since it seemed nothing could kill him! Another reference I used was of my uncle named John, who personifies his character well, and my partner, whose features fit for the pose.

BY EVE TUSHNET

The third day belongeth to St. John
Who was Christ's darling, dearer none.

That's a fifteenth-century English carol about the feasts after Christmas, including the feast of St. John, the Beloved Disciple, on December 27. His whole life is summed up in the phrase "Christ's darling." And that is what he always wanted. In the whole Gospel of John, there are two people who are never referred to by name: Mary is always "the mother of Jesus," and John himself is always "the disciple whom Jesus loved." It's as if he no longer even wants a name, he only wants people to know that Jesus loves him.

John's Gospel is the one with the most high-octane, straight-up weird depictions of Jesus: "the Word [who] became flesh" (John 1:14 NABRE), who "was in the beginning with God" (John 1:2 NABRE), the Word who is also "the true light, which enlightens everyone" (John 1:9 NABRE). And yet this Word and Light are also a person John knew and loved and touched. At the Last Supper, John rests against Jesus's breast. He lies there, gazing tenderly at the one whom he loves and who loves him. When the other disciples hesitate to ask Jesus which of them will betray Him, it's John who has the boldness to say what's on their minds. His physical intimacy with Jesus is like a visual representation of his openhearted honesty and trust.

The Gospel of John is like a microcosm of the Incarnation itself, uniting the most mysterious aspects of Jesus's life as the second person of the Trinity with the most down-to-earth aspects of His life as our tenderest friend.

At the cross all the men have fled—all except John. Jesus makes John and Mary kin to each other, telling Mary, "Woman, behold, your son," and John, "Behold, your mother" (John 19:26, 27 NABRE). The warmth of family and the wildness of celibacy unite here. The love, comfort, and support of kinship that we need in this life meet the radical witness to the love beyond "marrying and giving in marriage" (paraphrase of Matt. 22:30) that we will know in the next life.

These are only a few aspects of John's life. But they're the ones that have been most important to me. I love the mystical wildness of John's Gospel—the world is created by the Word, so everything you see is a poem. And I need the gentle intimacy and practical care of friends and family—and friends who become chosen family.

John's Gospel also speaks to me as a lesbian who seeks to live in harmony with the teachings of the Catholic Church. Since coming out to myself, I have known that being gay is about a longing for love and intimacy, not solely a longing for sex. But I didn't think that the Church had any models for that love and intimacy—for a life shaped by love of someone of the same sex. Slowly I've discovered that Scripture and Church history present the beauty of same-sex love and offer ways for us to become kin to people of the same sex. So many gay Christians have felt that Jesus was their judge and not their friend, that He had only condemnation for their longings rather than guidance. So many of us have felt like giving up sex to follow Jesus means giving up love, family, care, self-gift, and joy. Discovering the love John and Jesus shared has helped me to re-understand my own experience of both love and celibacy—and unite them.

Today, Christians—especially gay Christians—are rediscovering forgotten models of same-sex love and kinship and creating new models that meet contemporary needs. I have friends in "celibate partnerships," drawing inspiration from monasticism. I have friends who have taken vows of friendship or had their friendships blessed. For a long time I was sure that wouldn't be my path—my closest friendships were life-giving, but in a normal BFF way. My best friend isn't Catholic. We love each other, but in the way where you say, "We're going to be the Golden Girls one day," or "Here is another stuffed squid, because one time you were super annoying about a squid and now it's your nickname."

Then I met a Catholic woman who has shown me new dimensions of the tender, nonjudgmental, ardent love of Christ. Now we are figuring out whether we are called to become kin to each other, to share our lives in obedient faith and passionate love. I don't know if I would have recognized the love she was offering if I didn't have models like John's burning love of Jesus. When I lean against her breast, I hope I always think of him—and of his Divine Beloved.

PRAYER

Darling John, you know what it is like to be loved by Jesus. Pray for me so that I can know Him as intimately as you do. Darling John, you know what it is like to love Jesus—and to see His face in the outcast and despised. Pray for me so that I can stand beside you, and them, as Jesus's friend. Darling John, you know what it is like to feel the Sacred Heart beating as you lean back against your Lord. Pray for me so that I can rest beside you in Jesus's love.

EVE TUSHNET is the author of *Gay and Catholic* and *Tenderness: A Gay Christian's Guide to Unlearning Rejection and Experiencing God's Extravagant Love,* as well as two novels, *Amends* and *Punishment: A Love Story.* She lives in her hometown of Washington, DC. Her hobbies include sin, confession, and ecstasy.

BORN: **~18 B.C.**

DIED: **~33 A.D.**

FEAST: **MARCH 25**

PATRON OF FORGIVENESS, SECOND CHANCES, CRIMINALS, PRISONERS, ABOLITION OF CAPITAL PUNISHMENT

THE SHORT STORY—Dismas is the name given to the thief crucified on Jesus's right. Luke's Gospel tells us that while they were on the cross, one thief made fun of Jesus and mocked him while the other defended him and said,

> Have you no fear of God, for you are subject to the same condemnation? And indeed, we have been condemned justly, for the sentence we received corresponds to our crimes, but this man has done nothing criminal. Jesus, remember me, when you come into your kingdom. (Luke 23:40–49 NIV)

Jesus tells him in response that he will indeed be with him in Paradise. Interpretations of this passage have noted that this response makes Dismas the only confirmed saint—the only person we can know for sure is in Heaven, because Jesus said so. Neither history nor the Gospels give us any more information about him, though his name in Greek means "sunset" or "death,"

ARTIST'S STATEMENT—Dismas looks up to his left where Jesus would have been on the cross, as always depicted in Crucifixion images. Because he was said to have been tied to the cross rather than nailed, his clothing is made of ropes. The colors of the image and his tattoos are reminiscent of desert imagery, and the orange background represents his "sunset" namesake. He has a tattoo of the three crosses as well as ancient Hebrew pictograms.

and tradition holds that he was a thief who lived in the desert. In representations of the Crucifixion, Dismas and his thieving partner are usually shown as tied with rope to their crosses rather than nailed, while Jesus's head and/or feet are turned to his right as a symbolic acceptance of Dismas. St. Augustine wrote of Dismas with praise, and wondered if he was baptized at some point in his life despite his criminal career. There is also a medieval story about Dismas and his partner holding up the Holy Family on their flight to Egypt. In this story Dismas even then recognized something special about the family and paid off the other thieves to allow the trio safe passage.

BY ELISE CRAWFORD GALLAGHER

Have you ever felt like you don't belong? At various times throughout my faith journey, I've struggled with the feeling of being out of place as a Catholic. I come from a home where my mom was a practicing Catholic but my dad was an atheist. When talking to my peers whose families were seemingly harmonious and whose parents were both devout Christians, I felt like they were speaking a language that I never learned. Daily mass? Praying together as a family? The rosary? Liturgical living? All of these were foreign concepts to me during my adolescence.

While at university I experienced a return that led me into a deeper relationship with Jesus. I started attending daily mass, practicing the sacraments with vigor, and fell in love with my faith. At the same time my husband and I developed a beautiful relationship founded on a mutual desire to pursue sainthood.

After I graduated from college and moved into my career, I founded a marketing agency and fell in love with the world of business. Seeing a need for resources for Catholic women professionals, I eventually founded the organization Catholic Women in Business. In the last two years my husband and I welcomed two beautiful baby girls into our family, and I began navigating the reality of being a working mother.

Once again I felt out of place: I didn't fit in exactly with the stay-at-home moms at my parish (it's difficult to make a 10:00 A.M. play-date work during the week), but I also couldn't fully relate to my work colleagues who did not subscribe to a faith tradition. I felt like I didn't belong. I loved being a wife and mother, while I still felt called to work outside of the home. I enjoyed homemaking and yet knew that my business was a force for good in the world. Fortunately, over time the Lord has provided friendships and mentors who share my passion for business and my Catholic faith.

I believe we've all felt "out of place" at some point in our lives. When I meditate upon the experience of St. Dismas, I can't help thinking that this man was an outcast. We don't know much about him, but we do know he was a fugitive. He was abandoned and condemned to a gruesome death.

As St. Dismas hung next to Jesus on his own cross, what was he thinking? Had he encountered Jesus before? Had he heard about Jesus from a friend? What led to the moment when he declared with great surrender and clarity: "Jesus, remember me when you come into your kingdom"?

We might not know the answers to these questions, but we can certainly relate to St. Dismas's longing for Christ's mercy. The Sacred Heart of Jesus Christ is our home. Although we might feel outcast at certain times in our lives, we can always find belonging in the heart of our Savior, just as St. Dismas found rest in him during a moment of great suffering.

The truth is, we are not defined by our work, our social status, our state in life, or our hobbies. As Christians, we are defined by Christ's love for us. At our very core we are sons and daughters of a God whose love we do not have to earn or strive for. It is offered freely to us without hesitation by our Savior.

Jesus offered St. Dismas profound acceptance, acceptance that we all are gifted freely. Whenever I have felt at a loss, whether it's through the transition of having a new baby, moving, or making changes in my professional life, St. Dismas reminds me that Jesus doesn't ask me to have it "all figured out." He offers me a place to belong, a place where I can be myself.

In 1855 Ven. Fr. Augustine Marie of the Most Blessed Sacrament mourned the loss of his mother, Rosalee Cohan. She never converted to his Catholic faith from her Jewish roots and he wondered whether she would be in Heaven. Six years later he received a letter from a Jesuit friend that contained a miraculous revelation: Jesus had communicated to a holy woman in prayer that through Mary's intercession, moments from death, Rosalee's soul had been saved anyway.[12]

Fr. Augustine Marie's revelation highlights St. Dismas's own experience on the cross: that it's never too late. It is never too late for change or radical conversion, and what's more, nothing is too big or too far gone for God to save. Even though we may identify as faithful Catholics, it's easy to be discouraged by our own failings and lack of faith. We can look to St. Dismas to be reminded of the truth: we are truly never lost. Our God is a God of mystery and miracles.

Let us ask for St. Dismas's intercession to humbly come before the Lord in our weakness and our imperfection and receive his boundless love and mercy. May we always seek our true identity in our Creator and boldly live our faith so that one day we may hear the words from Christ: "Truly, I say to you, today you will be with Me in Paradise" (Luke 23:43 NIV).

PRAYER

St. Dismas, thank you for your example of meekness of heart. I ask that you help me to see my identity as a son or daughter of God. Help me to live authentically this truth and let it permeate my thoughts, words, and actions. May we always find a home within the Church and Christ's Sacred Heart. St. Dismas, walk with us on this journey of faith and grant us hope of our Savior's mercy. Strengthen our belief. We ask this through the intercession of our Blessed Mother always. Amen.

ELISE CRAWFORD GALLAGHER is the founder and CEO of RINGLET. Created in 2017, RINGLET has produced national, multilevel campaigns for startups around the country. In 2018 she cofounded the Catholic Women in Business community, which offers articles, networking, and virtual events to Catholic women looking to integrate their faith into their work life. Elise is married to her college sweetheart, and they live with their two daughters in Maryland.

ST. BERNADETTE

ARTIST'S STATEMENT—One of the references for this portrait was a roommate of mine who had chosen Bernadette as her Confirmation saint. I wanted her eyes to convey the otherworldly things St. Bernadette had seen. I also wanted her expression to be one of confidence in herself despite pressure—something in which my roommate also excelled.

BORN: **JANUARY 7, 1844**

DIED: **APRIL 16, 1879**

FEAST: **APRIL 16**

PATRON OF SHEPHERDS, ILLNESS, LOURDES, PEOPLE RIDICULED FOR THEIR FAITH, POVERTY, ASTHMA

THE SHORT STORY—Bernadette was born into an impoverished family, and she became very sick with asthma, cholera, and other ailments when she was young. When she was fourteen she, a friend, and her younger sister went to gather firewood. As they were walking home, Bernadette saw a bright light illuminating a cave and a figure in white and blue. She returned to the cave, alone, twenty times because the woman in her vision had asked her to. During one of her visits Bernadette had an encounter in which the apparition asked her to drink and wash in the water there, and the next day the filthy water ran clear. Her family was so embarrassed about Bernadette's trips to the cave that they tried to keep her from going. Bernadette was interrogated by the Catholic Church and French government officials, and in 1862 it was finally declared that she had been speaking the truth and she had seen Mary, the mother of God. She asked a local priest to build a chapel at the cave, where people could come and wash in the water. Bernadette joined a religious order before contracting tuberculosis.

BY JESSICA GERHARDT

My grandma Barbie had a very colorful past. She was a teen mom in the 1950s, a divorcée before she turned twenty, a flirt, a smoker, a drinker, and a truck driver who loved to dance and party. Surely some of her debauchery was a reaction to growing up in an alcoholic and dysfunctional household, leaving an abusive marriage and becoming a single mom, and the Catholic Church's unwillingness to grant her an annulment until after Vatican II. Nevertheless, toward the end of her life she became very devout in her faith. Her honesty and willingness to take responsibility for her past and mistakes, coupled with her deep love of Jesus and trust in God's love for her, were formative in my own faith development.

Despite their differences, my grandmother felt deeply connected to Bernadette of Lourdes, and she was the person who introduced me to this saint. With the reminders of her periodic gifts of small plastic grotto-shaped water bottles at Christmas and Easter, I became intrigued by the story of Bernadette and the miracle at Lourdes. During one of her visits my grandmother introduced my mom, my sister, and me to the classic film *Song of Bernadette,* which swept the Golden Globes and Academy Awards in 1944. I was so moved by it and how beautifully it depicted Bernadette's life.

Bernadette was a young woman from an impoverished family; she battled poor health and didn't have much education because she missed school so often due to her illnesses. She was otherwise a fairly ordinary girl. Yet God chose her to be an instrument by which he revealed a major theological concept for the Church. When Mary appeared to her and told her "I am the Immaculate Conception," Bernadette didn't even know what that meant! In some ways it was her ignorance that led others to believe her. Though at first many in her community were skeptical of her visions and encounters with Mary, Bernadette remained true to herself and her faith.

The miracle at the grotto is also of tremendous significance to me. Our Lady of Lourdes told Bernadette to dig in the ground and drink and wash her face in the water of the spring that would come forth. In the film *Song of Bernadette,* Bernadette digs in the ground and there's barely any water, so she begins to wipe her face with mud. The scene has stayed with me to this day. That kind of faithfulness would seem to all others a great foolishness, perhaps even an insanity. Yet Bernadette follows what she knows to be true, and just as Our Lady told her, a clear spring burst forth from that place. Since then Lourdes has become one of the most visited Catholic pilgrimage sites in the world. The miracles in the lives of those who have waded in or been sprinkled with its waters are countless. All because one young woman stayed true to her conscience and followed the invitations of God despite how unusual they seemed.

Like Bernadette, my grandma didn't have much formal education and she battled many health issues throughout her life. Yet she also remained true to herself and to her faith, even to her last days on earth. Part of me struggles with feeling different from others, and I fear what others will think of me; sometimes I compare my life to someone else's and feel discouraged about where I'm at. The other part of me is drawn to nonconformity and wants to be unique, marching to the beat of my own drum, but that can often feel lonely. I can only imagine the strength of character Bernadette had in order to persevere in her own truth when Church authorities, and even her own family, doubted her. I imagine that her own deep sense of God's presence, and her intimate friendships with Jesus and Mary, gave her consolation even when she battled public ridicule and physical frailty.

I think about the ways that one life like Bernadette's (as brief as it was, only thirty-five years) can touch so many others, and the similarity to the way my grandma's life (though she passed away at age seventy-nine) continues to impact mine. I even wrote a song about the inspiration I take from her life.*

The point is, whether a person's life is long or short, and whether they become famous or remain relatively unknown, that life touches others in countless ways, both seen and unseen—and in ways they may never know. While we don't know the hour when our lives on earth will end, we can choose how we live out the gift

* What a woman, and oh what a past, well you owned it all with a side-eye glance and a laugh . . . Who am I without you in this world? Who can I call when I feel alone? . . . I know you laid it all in His hands, so that's where I'll go, when I need to know . . . you're with me.

(Lyrics from "Keep It Simple," available on all streaming platforms.)

of each day. I hope that, following in the footsteps of St. Bernadette and of my grandma, I will continue to look to Jesus's friendship even when I feel like the path I'm walking is lonely, and that I will continue to remain true to the path I am uniquely called to walk with God.

PRAYER

Lord, help us to trust that you're with us as we seek to walk in our authentic truth. Help us to remember that our worth and value are in you, not in the eyes or opinions of others. Help us to be honest about our failings but to be gentle with ourselves as we consider your abundant love, mercy, and invitation to deep friendship. Help us to follow in the footsteps of Bernadette, to stay true to our faith and vocations, even when doing so seems foolish and the path may feel lonely. St. Bernadette of Lourdes, pray for us. Amen.

JESSICA GERHARDT is a singer-songwriter, worship musician, artist, rosary maker, and writer originally from Santa Monica, California. You can listen to her music on all streaming platforms and follow her @jgerhardtmusic (Twitter/Instagram) and @workofhumanhandsart (IG) or go to www.jessicagerhardt.com.

ST. BRENDAN

ARTIST'S STATEMENT—With a sailor's jacket emblazoned with the shamrock of his country, a St. Brendan's cross, and a compass around his neck, Brendan is ready for wherever his journeys will take him. His eyes are wide with wonder, maybe a little fear, and most of all, admiration for the beautiful creation he encountered.

BORN: **484**

DIED: **577**

FEAST: **MAY 16**

PATRON OF SAILING, SHIPS, WHALES, DIVERS, TRAVELERS, NAVIGATION

THE SHORT STORY—At age six Brendan was sent to a monastery school, and he was ordained a priest at age twenty-six. He made it his mission to establish monasteries around the world, and that intention is what took him on voyages to the Scottish Islands, Wales, and the coast of France. Legend has it that he set sail with fourteen to seventeen other monks on a seven-year journey to find the Garden of Eden. It is thought that he could have been eighty years old when he took this expedition. *Navigatio Sancti Brendani Abbatis* (*Voyage of Saint Brendan the Abbot*), written around the year 900, tells the legend of what transpired on this voyage. It was thought that Brendan made it to Greenland, Iceland, and possibly Jamaica, the Bahamas, and North America. Many have suggested he could have been the first European in the Americas. After establishing a few more monasteries and churches locally, Brendan died while visiting his sister in Annaghdown, Ireland. His last words to her were that he would now have to journey alone to a very unknown land.

BY SARAH QUINT

If you find it hard to believe in picnics on the backs of whales, islands of giant sheep, prophetic birds, and transatlantic leather canoe voyages like the ones in Brendan's story, then perhaps you will understand just how hard it is for an Indigenous person to believe in Christians who come to our shores carrying good intentions. But this is indeed the story of St. Brendan, a fifth-century

Irish monk who ventured to the shores of Turtle Island (North America) in an oak-and-tanned-leather canoe, and this is also mine. I am a Native woman of Turtle Island, from the epicenter of English-first-contact. Against many odds I deeply love Creator-Sets-Free (Jesus), and I follow the Jesus Way.

I first heard of St. Brendan while talking to a dear friend, Jarrod McKenna, who is from an Irish Catholic family. He introduced me to the story of St. Brendan and his men, who traveled without causing harm and who believed in the inherent goodness of my place and people. The story predates the colonization of both Ireland and Turtle Island. These voyagers arrived as foreign family, and we shared many commonalities. Both Irish and First Nations people love to tell a good story, to spin a yarn, leaving many to question "Is this real?" But what our tales lack in facts they make up for in truth. And St. Brendan's larger-than-life witness provides both an ancient way forward and a commentary on what could have been.

I approached St. Brendan with the mistrust I was born into. Reading everything about him I could get my hands on, I deeply wanted to believe him. As I read, he came to feel less like a fairy tale and more like a prayer to me. He embodied what I hoped human interactions could be throughout the earth. How different would the lives of Indigenous people around the world be today if everyone who carried the name of Christ in their travels did so in the manner of St. Brendan the Navigator?

Many who came to our shores believed this continent was theirs to discover and possess. With the Doctrine of Discovery and Manifest Destiny in hand, cosigned by the European Church, a worldwide race and many wars ensued to procure this grand prize, the land. Once during his voyage, Brendan encountered a great sea monster. My people too have firsthand experience with sea monsters, who broke loose from the pages of fairy tales and brought apocalyptic devastation to our home. St. Brendan was no such monster. Where some saw *terra nullius,* Brendan saw the "Isle of the Blessed," filled with those bearing Earth Maker's image.

The journey was treacherous for St. Brendan and his men, but the Great Spirit was with them along the way. They traveled with humility, and at each stop they made, they asked permission to be there. Brendan and his men took only what was needed and nothing more. Prayerful gratitude was expressed with every gift. Their quest was founded not on greedy intent or conquest but only the desire to know more of God. If Eden is the place where Heaven and Earth meet, where Creator walks with the two-legged in the cool of the day, then St. Brendan was correct in calling our lands the Isle of Paradise. We were not godless savages. No! This place was Eden and we were its holy inhabitants. Without ever leaving earth, the travelers had seen Heaven. I want to trust that God's shores can still bring good things, like the salmon's faithful return.

As subjugated people we have no choice but to know the infamous names of Christopher Columbus, Captain James Cook, and Captain Samuel Argall. But few know the likes of St. Brendan and his seafaring saints. Like good guests they came quietly, left no devastation in their wake, and made it easy for us to forget they were ever here. One's adventures should never reverberate through generations. Today many people take vacations to remote Indigenous spaces. They use travel as an excuse to reserve morality for home while they pollute the land and exploit the people. St. Brendan encourages us to be faithful travelers who never abandon the way of Christ as we leave home.

One of the more powerful things about Brendan's story is that he came home. If he were alive today, perhaps he would greatly commission travelers to "return and tell" the good news that God can be found throughout the world. His story challenges us to remember what it is like to be good hosts and good guests. It begs the questions What is hospitality without distrust? and What is travel without harm?

PRAYER

Creator, protect us from enemies who seek to harm. Make them like ancient boundary stones, unable to move from their mark.

Let no foreign land know your people as enemies. We reject spoils taken by greed and accept only the gifts received through relationship. Restore the trampled tables of hospitality so we can live openhearted and openhanded once again. Guard our hearts against hardening toward the sojourner. Looking to Christ, we prepare a place for all. In our travels, may we never carry your name in vain. Let our comings and goings be marked with humility and reciprocity, producing friends, not enemies. Expand our faith until we anticipate finding you in every corner of the earth. Let us refuse to believe in the "godless place." Following St. Brendan's example, teach us to walk gently across the land, as good guests with good hearts. As we arrive, may we confess, "Surely the Lord is in this place." Amen.

SARAH QUINT (Mattaponi) practices a decolonized and contextual faith in Jesus through traditional storytelling and songwriting in her tribal language. Her work in the church is to prophetically call the people of Christ out of harmful colonial ways and into the freedom found in the Kingdom of God. Sarah is the colead Pastor of Monroe City Church in Monroe, Michigan (Potawatomi Territory).

ST. HILDEGARD OF BINGEN

BIRTH: **1098**

DEATH: **SEPTEMBER 17, 1179**

FEAST: **SEPTEMBER 17**

PATRON OF WRITERS, DOCTORS, HEALERS, SCIENTISTS, COMPOSERS, PLAYWRIGHTS, ARTISTS, WOMEN LEADERS AND SPEAKERS, FEMINISTS, OPERAS, THE ENVIRONMENT AND CONSERVATION

THE SHORT STORY—When Hildegard was eighteen, she entered a religious community, and twenty years later she was elected the leader of the women's convent. Hildegard decided that she needed to move her growing community to a new location and, against fierce opposition from the powers that be in the Church, founded a monastery of her own. She was forty-two years old when she began writing her book *Scivias.* Despite her lack of formal education, she became extremely well versed in natural science and medicinal plants for healing. She composed music, operas, and what is considered the first morality play. Hildegard also broke social and geopolitical barriers by traveling extensively throughout Germany, preaching in public places, writing letters to royal and authority figures, and inventing her own alphabet. Hildegard used her preaching tours to call out corruption, abuse of power, and indifference to the needs of oth-

ARTIST'S STATEMENT—How could I possibly fit all of Hildegard's wide range of talents and vast influence into one portrait? Her earbud is symbolic of her musical talent, the plants in her pocket are symbolic of her scientific and medical knowledge, and the pen is a symbol of her art and writing. Her female symbol tattoo is representative of the boundaries she crossed for women and her "flame" eye shadow serves as a symbol of her visions. This extraordinary woman is clearly concentrating—on what, at the moment, it is impossible to tell, but she is about to change history. She is a role model to all of us who worry about inadequacy, but we can see all she was able to accomplish once she overcame that fear.

ers. In addition, she spoke out against social class division, rallied for gender equality, and advocated for holistic healing and mental health. She also wrote about the Divine Feminine and woman's extremely important place in nature and Christianity. She is now a Doctor of the Church.

BY MEGHAN TSCHANZ

It was 2016 and I felt like the world was crumbling around me. I had spent the previous year begging and pleading with the white evangelical Church to not do what I had always known them to do: vote for the Republican candidate—regardless of their policies, character, or words. I had always rebuffed the Christian-equals-Republican narrative and voted for Barack Obama in my first-ever presidential election, but this time voting for the Republican candidate meant something other than choosing between differing partisan ideologies.

Trump ran his campaign on othering and alienating people whom Jesus commanded us to love. And still, white evangelicals showed up en masse to vote for him. I spent the day after the election sobbing at the mission's organization where I work. A trusted man called me into his office and said, "Someday, Meghan, you will see this is God's will."

As a survivor of sexual assault myself, and as a woman who had spent the last several years as a missionary working with female survivors of sexual assault and sex trafficking, I could not reconcile this "God" that white evangelicals knew with the God that I knew—the One who sat and wept and raged with righteous indignation at what had happened to us.

When I shared online that I had voted for Hillary Clinton instead of Trump, the messages of hatred started pouring in. People told me that I was going to Hell, that they were praying for my soul, and that we could not possibly worship the same Jesus—on that they may have been right.

I decided that if these people were going to represent a Jesus who loved money and power, cast immigrants as murderers and rapists, and turned a blind eye to sexual assault, then I was going to share a different Jesus: the one I knew, whose love was uncontainable, who brought those from the margins in, and who deeply and passionately cared for women.

I quit my job, started a podcast bent on reclaiming feminism for the Christian faith called *Faith and Feminism,* and wrote a book calling out the Church's complicity with patriarchy and how it harmed women the world over.

At first I felt terribly alone. Challenging the Church meant losing friends and family, and it felt like I was forging a path that had never been walked before. But I had a deep conviction in my veins that this was what God had called me to do.

It wasn't until midway through my journey that I discovered the Church has a rich and robust history of saints, and even women saints, who had forged paths similar to mine. One such saint, Hildegard of Bingen, sounded like she knew what it was to call out patriarchy and corrupt power in the Church centuries before I arrived on the scene.

She became known for her fiery speeches, in which she did not shy away from calling out corrupt religious leaders, authorities who abused their power, and the religious elite who sat back and enjoyed their wealth and status instead of getting into the communities to minister to those Christ commanded us to serve. She spoke out against social class divisions, railed against gender inequity, and advocated for holistic healing, which involved caring for both physical and mental health. She was perhaps the first writer to speak about women's sexuality in a positive light, writing the first description of the female orgasm.[13] She also had visions of air pollution and deforestation that would devastate the planet and advocated that we as humans take care of the land we live on.

As I read her story and her words, I can't help but feel so much less alone. For centuries women have been naming and protesting the complicity of the Church with the unjust power systems that be. It is not a sin to do this; in fact, women who did so often became holy saints.

I imagine that if St. Hildegard were alive today, she too would be chastising the white evangelical Church and the injustice of its aligning with power and prestige rather than with the very people Christ commanded us to care about.

When I read Hildegard's story, I remember I'm not alone. I am just another woman called by God to make this world a more just and equitable place.

PRAYER

God, give us the eyes to see the systems and history we were born into. Help us to lament and repent where we need to, and work toward a more equitable world. Give us the courage to stand up to our friends and family who still support systems of injustice, give us grace and humility as we navigate a better way forward. And help us always to remember that we are not alone, that you have called us for such a time as this.

MEGHAN TSCHANZ is the author of *Women Rising* and the host of the much-loved *Faith and Feminism* podcast. After growing up in the conservative evangelical Church, she came to a reckoning with her upbringing while serving as a missionary working with exploited women. Since then she has been set on dismantling harmful systems within our faith. She and her husband live with their little girl and two rescue dogs in Athens, Georgia.

ST. PEREGRINE

ARTIST'S STATEMENT—Peregrine is clearly under stress in this image, not only from his physical pain but from not being able to work and help others in the way he is used to. His face has a look of questioning God about this pain, and his walking cane rests beside him as if he has fallen just a moment before.

BORN: **1265**

DIED: **MAY 1, 1345**

FEAST: **MAY 1**

PATRON OF CANCER, AIDS, TERMINAL ILLNESSES

THE SHORT STORY—Peregrine was the only son of a wealthy family in Forli, Italy. When he was a teenager, he became very politically active in his community. He and his family were part of an anti-papal group of which Peregrine himself was the leader. Soon Pope Martin IV punished the group for their rebelliousness and placed Forli under an interdict closing all of its churches. When the group did not abide by the censure, the Pope sent St. Philip Benizi to try to prevent an uprising. While Philip was addressing the citizens, Peregrine, who was then eighteen, and his group pulled Philip off of his platform, made fun of him, and beat him, Peregrine himself striking Philip violently in the face. Later, remorseful about his act, Peregrine sought out Philip to apologize, and he was greatly moved when the man, who had every right to be angry, met him with kindness and forgiveness instead. Philip's response to Peregrine's ill treatment had such an impact on Peregrine that he changed his political and theological ideals and joined the Servite Order in Siena. Peregrine made it his mission to help the impoverished and sick members of his community; he became a priest and later founded his own Servite house. He was greatly loved by the people he served and was known for saying, "Better today than yesterday, better tomorrow than today!" He was also known to give good advice, and he loved preaching. He was even reputed to have performed a miracle when his area experienced a famine and he was able to multiply grain and wine. A few years after Peregrine founded his own monastery he was diagnosed with cancer in his right leg.

When a horribly painful wound appeared, it was decided that his leg needed to be amputated. The night before he was to be operated on, however, Peregrine prayed unceasingly until he fell asleep. He dreamed of Jesus touching the diseased spot on his leg. In the morning the surgeon could find no trace of the cancer. The people of Forli, after learning of this miraculous cure, began to come to Peregrine for healing, which he was often able to accomplish with Divine help.

BY ABBY ELLIS

Scripture says it is the kindness of God that leads us to repentance, and it was the confounding tenderness of St. Philip Benizi that earned him a follower in Peregrine, who was converted not by mandate, shame, or force. And following that encounter with Benizi, Peregrine gave his life not to a system, authority, or empire but to honorable men connected to Benizi who lived and served in proximity to the most marginalized. Often whispering the name of Jesus in the ears of the poor, Peregrine became known as an angel of good counsel and wisdom.

How is it that this young man of violence was later described as wise? As a mother and trauma-informed therapist, I'm often curious about anger and aggression. These primal emotions are often responses to threat, shame, and hurt. They are frequently attempts to protect and preserve the self, the brain's brilliant efforts to guard against further violation or the relinquishment of free will. I'm equally intrigued when the same angry and resistant individuals learn how to soften and settle. What I know is that often this soothing comes through the safe and kind presence of another. It comes through attunement that communicates belonging and value. Could it be that Peregrine's saintliness was rooted in the angry resistance he displayed? To be sure, Peregrine was schooled by those above him; from some he learned scarcity and demand that required a response of self-preservation and defense. But from another he learned safety and acceptance despite his unholy presentation. In that moment Peregrine did not relinquish his God-given sense of justice, his righteous anger, or his desire to serve those among him. Instead he was provoked by peace and invited to a new way of being. Safe and acceptable in the eyes of Benizi, he refused the allure of rage and contempt and chose, in their place, the radical way of love. This looked like a lifetime of service in the streets, often standing first to feed, pray with, and clothe his neighbors. At the day's end he was the last to sit; some believe this daily decision was an instigating cause of his cancer.

Could it be that a single man who chooses from a heart that has been won is more effective in the Kingdom than a hundred who resist and concede? Transformation happens in the particularity of a person's life. Shifts in understanding happen when people are engaged by others in critical moments of sadness, anger, fear, loneliness, and grief. Therefore, true conversion must be deeply personal, individualized, and incremental. Change that lasts occurs in the kind of proximity that reads the nuance of a face, sees a subtle shift in posture, perceives the rise and fall of a chest, and notices a clenched fist. It begins with being seen and feeling known. Often the body relaxes, the shoulders drop, the countenance softens, and sometimes there are tears. Occasionally there is laughter. Truth that lands in the brain and gut of a person, who is not merely a soul but a mind and a body too, looks nothing like humiliation, defeat, submission, or performance. Truth that heals looks like love. Truth that transforms looks like rest, with no requirement to hide out, fight back, or flee. When truth takes, it looks a lot like waking up.

Peregrine's miraculous story often centers on the healing of his cancer. But I've come to believe that he was battling a sort of cultural cancer long before malignancy appeared on his leg. To simplify the healing of his wound is to simplify the wound itself. For what is cancer but an explicit sign to the whole body that all is not well on the inside? Health, at its most fundamental level, has gone awry. I don't believe Peregrine's time was so unlike our own—with Church, state, politics, and people deeply divided, threatened, grieved, exhausted, and disconnected. But if it's true that there is *nothing new under the sun,* then we know that cancer in the Body (of Christ) looks a lot like cancer in the body.

I've seen cancer win and lose. I've seen it taunt and sometimes flat-out take. Sometimes, despite our best demands, finest minds, and most aggressive responses, those cells simply won't submit. Sometimes cancer takes who and what we love most. Sometimes in the end it's hard to tell where good tissue begins and ends. We are simply left wishing for nearness, for a glance into the absent eyes of the one who knew us best. I've seen cancer steal life: a weeping wife in the ICU, a son singing his mother goodbye, a nephew with tumors, a sister-in-law with scars, a friend with impossible decisions. But in every cancer tale, proximity is the hero. Whether it be the laser-like closeness of therapeutic drugs or the presence of a comforting other. Coming close, whether in death or in life, is what changes people. I believe Peregrine's healing at the foot of a cross was indeed a miracle. But I believe even more in the miracle of a Christ who comes low and close in our wounded desperation, confusion, violence, anger, grief, self-righteousness, self-sabotage, and isolation.

I've suffered from my own forms of cancer: shame, contempt, hopelessness, and despair. These kinds can invade a soul, a mind, and a body until every cell screams of sickness. But I can name the date my countenance changed, the Sunday my heartache was acknowledged, and the night I danced in the mirror with a new posture and a new word of praise. I was changed by the kindness of strangers—the kind that leans in close to your open wound and asks you how it came to be. The kind that answered my resistance with a smile I believed.

In a small town in Italy at a time when there was no peace, young Peregrine refused to be lulled into submission by calls of "Peace, peace" when there was none. But he softened—this is what repentance is—without shame and with his free will intact. Benizi offered Peregrine mutuality instead of muscle. The healing of division began with a gaze into the wound, a movement toward the pain, the aggressor, the unknown, the other. Love is particular and persistent. Love confounds and disorients. Love rejects antiseptic amputation but insists on radical regeneration, one cell, one smile at a time. Love is unreasonable without reasonable cause because it is the kindness of God that leads us to repentance. Sometimes the wounded wound. Sometimes the wounded are healed. And sometimes the wounded are the healers.

PRAYER

St. Peregrine, as the patron saint of cancer, be with those of us and those we love who are afflicted by this terrible disease. Be with us and them in every pain, every loss, every frustration, every fear, and every loss of hope, for you know each of these. Bring healing and peace as you were granted, and be with us for every step of this journey.

Amen.

ABBY ELLIS is a wife, mom, daughter, sister, friend, and therapist. A lover of life, liturgy, words, and the Word. An insatiable seeker of everything, beauty hunter, deep breather, sad song repeater. A broken member of a broken body, making amends in the margins, breaking bread with the misfits, and coming back to life. A defiant holder of heartache, harm, and the hope of Kingdom Come, only right here and now—only just—as it is in Heaven.

ST. ZOE

BORN: **EARLY SECOND CENTURY**

DIED: **127**

FEAST: **MAY 2**

PATRON OF DOGS, MOTHERS, WIVES, FIRE

THE SHORT STORY—Zoe lived with her husband, Exsuperius, and had two sons, Cyriacus and Theodulus. They were a Christian family enslaved by a wealthy Roman. Zoe's job was to look after the dogs and keep them from biting people. It was also said that she worked near a road, and so when weary travelers walked by, she would give them some of her food, despite not having very much for herself. Legend also says that she and her husband were separated while working and did not often get to see each other. Upon the birth of their second son, in keeping with Roman tradition, they were given food to sacrifice to the Roman gods. When Zoe's family refused to participate in the offering, they were all tortured and burned alive in a furnace.

BY CARA MEREDITH

I chose St. Zoe of Pamphylia for a single reason: I knew her name means "life." That fact alone made up the reason for my choosing to write about her.

I didn't know a thing about the saint or her family.

And if I'm honest, the more I got to know St. Zoe, the more I wanted her story to be a little sexier, perhaps with a happier, more life-filled ending. I wanted a "saved from the fiery furnace," Shadrach,

ARTIST'S STATEMENT—In this icon Zoe carries the items of her two jobs—caring for dogs and caring for her children. Her identities as both mother and worker, however, are overshadowed by the bright, luminescent red that symbolizes her heart on fire with the Holy Spirit, as well as her fiery death.

Meshach, and Abednego type of story. I wanted her to have a widow's mite kind of provision, straight from Heaven above, or to see her sprinkled with extra coins by a chief tax collector who liked to climb trees in his spare time.

Really, I wanted to use my imagination to rewrite her story and make it more palatable to my taste. I suppose you could say I wanted to create a saint in my image and to my likeness—which is to admit that I didn't really want a saint after all.

Which is exactly why she is the saint for me.

Too often, I find myself trapped by what could be, unable to relish the desperate, begging beauty of the present. For me, the grass is always greener on the other side: if I can just get this job, then I'll be happy. If I can just start this writing project, then I'll really make it as an author. If I can just land this pitch, cement this relationship, cook this perfect dinner, then all the cards will fall into place.

If I can just . . . if I can just . . . if I can just.

I forget that Zoe offers another way: even in her servitude, she was present with others. She saw their needs and offered them her meager provisions. She wasn't always looking ahead, her mind already onto the next best thing, but she responded to the needs of the moment.

Years ago I heard a speaker address an auditorium full of high school students. He held a rope in his hands, slowly pulling its strands through his fingers. "Life is like this rope," he said. The rope traveled from one hand to the other, the entire braid of nylon pooling at his feet.

"Too often we think we've got an entire rope of a life left to live. But the truth is that our time on earth is only this much of the rope." The man found the start of the rope again, pinching his thumb and index finger around the first inch of its strands. "Our time on earth," he repeated, was only "this much" of the very long rope's length. The rest signified the amount of time we would someday spend in eternity.

He wanted us to make our one-inch time on earth matter in the long run, to make our one-inch life count.

In truth, I didn't accept all of the theological assertions offered that day. The man presented a "sinners in the hands of an angry God" type of invitation to live and abide by rules of righteousness—or else. His was a do-or-die kind of invitation to belief, a transactional claim that the love of God would be missed were we not to follow a certain version of the Christian faith.

But I never forgot that image of the rope.

As a seven on the Enneagram scale, I can too often go to the extremes to feel alive. I want my one-inch piece of life, and the many feet of rope that follow, to really, truly matter. Instead of accepting reality, I become so desirous of life itself that I romanticize a story that is not necessarily real and is not necessarily true.

I pick a saint at random. I take not the tragedy and sacrifice of her story, but I flip and twist it. I turn her into something she is not, caught up in my dreams of what could have been and should have been and very well might be someday in the future.

I forget to enter into the beauty of the present.

I forget to gaze into the life of someone like St. Zoe of Pamphylia and simply learn from her. But seeing as she's now been written on my soul, I imagine that has become my invitation. To make my life count, simply, right here and now.

PRAYER

God, you have given us the simple life of St. Zoe of Pamphylia. Although some called her the saint of nothing, to you she was everything. Teach us what it means to enter into the moment, accepting the reality of this one wild, precious life, as it is, and not make it into something it is not. Amen.

CARA MEREDITH is a chaser of beauty in the present, including into the lives of forgotten saints like St. Zoe of Pamphylia. As a freelance writer, editor, and coach, Cara is the author of *The Color of Life* and is also in the ordination process in the Episcopal Church. She lives with her family in Oakland, California.

MADONNA AND CHILD

MARIAN DEVOTION

THE SHORT STORY—The image of Mary holding baby Jesus has been popular since ancient times. It stresses her role as the mother not only of Jesus but of all of us.

BY CAMILLE HERNANDEZ

I gave life in waters three times
skin glistening in water lapped endurance
ebony hopes erupting life from womb-soil
hello, my sweet little baby
Their first journey: my birth canal
Their first baptism: my waters
Their first praise dance: cardinal movements of labor
Birth is crucible:
bloody, torturous,
exhausting, *eventual* joy
my pelvis, their torana // their crown, my blood
I am Madonna with child

My Aunty lost her child before I was born
Every day she sends a text message, solid
-ified unbreakable bond between aunty and niece

ARTIST'S STATEMENT—Because this icon is a companion piece to the Holy Family, I wanted the warm, loving, divine gold, and the spiritual, ethereal blue echoed in its colors. Mary's jeans are ripped from navigating the long journey to Bethlehem while pregnant. She has on her sweatshirt to be comfortable and keep away the night's cold. She has wrapped Jesus in the nicest piece of clothing she brought with her; and she has a tattoo of her immaculate heart on her wrist. Jesus touches her, either with joy or with pain, and she feels either peace or fear, depending on the viewer's needs and ideas.

At thirty-two I finally spoke my truth about childhood scars
her ears, the first to listen,
on the receiving end of that phone
I will never forget her deep breath and plain truth
"I don't care if it's your dad, your boyfriend, your brother, or whoever—
No one is allowed to talk to you or treat you like that anymore."
She is the Madonna and I am the child

My best friend, not yet thirty, had twenty-five babies
each one a newborn foster baby with their own story.
She sings hope, collects pictures, curates albums
just like her babies they are gifted away
In the moments she has them
before the heartbreak separation
She stays up all night, planting verses in their little souls.
Holding their newly born bodies during drug withdrawal.
Sometimes she's sleepless;
sometimes she cries.
every time she is *mommy*
She is Madonna with child(ren).

My siblingfriend facilitates community healing
Queer, Black, and non-Black people of color can live outside heteronormativity's obsessive murderous gaze
conjuring Holy Spirit healing magic
reclaiming every beloved thing
spiritual abuse locusts stole
ushering people, embracing blessed identities
no longer criticized
suppressed or
beaten out of them.
A glory it is to watch towers of Babel fall: those years of
cutting words, false accusations, godless abuse
slowly untethered. tangle us anew,
knot new hope into our reality, call it *re*parenting
Madonna with child(ren)

There is a moment in childbirth called "hitting the moon"
After the baby is born, the body exists beyond exhaustion
from pushing & straining & screaming & crying
there is no energy left to give
oxytocin the miracle rushing through each cell sustaining.
Watch newborn baby arm-cradled for the first time
glimpse of home
eye to eye
tears to forehead
perhaps relief perhaps love perhaps
pain
yes, it's motherhood
Indescribable joy soothes lacerations
It feels like . . .
"we made it"
"we did it"
"hello"
the sheer luck of love keeping all alive

it doesn't look like C-sections or vaginal births.
It is . . .
kitchen table conversations with aunty
sleepless nights with detoxing babies
embracing the belovedness of a marginalized
identity

I am still finding sacred motherhood beyond biology.
It is not owned by hierarchy (but we don't diminish our roles)
instead
Madonna removes the veil of
power
embodying care-centered leadership
to find the Madonna and child
seek one liturgy: restorative relationship.

I ask you this . . .

Who is your Madonna?

Who is your child?

PRAYER

Mother God,

Cradle us in loving embrace, let us hear your heartbeat and breathe to its rhythm. Nourish our withered souls. Let the warmth of your presence emanate into our relationships. Alchemize yourself into the building blocks of our healing communities. Kiss us with your kindness. Remind us that we are so cared for by you that we can cry out. We need help validating these cries for help. We need help knowing that we are worthy of care. Will you be here to help us hold each other as the Madonna embraces Jesus? Teach us to tend to wounded souls with as much care as Mary remedying the Messiah's scraped knee. Do not let us be motherless. Do not let us be desolate. Do not leave us alone. For it is Your Eternal Love we seek and alchemize into liberation. We need you as we survive this moment. Interpret our cries in the ways that mothering teaches us to do. Instill into our memories that mothering is not limited to biology but that your mothering Spirit goes forth with us when we build community and family and safety and liberation for targeted, disenfranchised, and hurting peoples. Mama, we need you. Amen.

CAMILLE HERNANDEZ is a theopoet, community healer, and podcaster fusing her talents to help people develop practices to reduce harm and invite flourishing. She's the host of the *O Heaux-ly Night* Advent podcast devotional and cohost of the *Abolition as Resurrection* Lenten podcast. You can find her on Twitter, Instagram, and TikTok as @hellocamilleh.

ST. SIMEON STYLITES THE YOUNGER

ARTIST'S STATEMENT—With the symbol of a pillar on his sweatshirt, Simeon wears dreadlocks, woven to minimize upkeep, and he has a grown-out beard for the same reason. With no time to dedicate to anything other than prayer, and with few supplies and amenities with which to perform regular grooming, Simeon looks only to the sky, symbolized by the blue color scheme.

BORN: **521**

DIED: **MAY 24, 597**

FEAST: **MAY 24**

PATRON OF HEIGHTS, SOLITUDE, ASCETICISM

THE SHORT STORY—Simeon was born in Antioch in what is modern-day Turkey. His father died when he was five years old. He was then entrusted to the care of a monk named John, who became his closest friend. When Simeon was just seven years old, he and John built pillars inspired by his namesake, the first Simeon Stylites. The two lived atop their pillars to ensure peace in their prayer and contemplation. Though they built the pillars to find solitude, word spread about their unusual lifestyle and extraordinary devotion to prayer, and pilgrims came to visit the men. Simeon, who was then twenty years old, came down from his pillar, and to avoid visitors, he left to hide in the mountains. Several years later Simeon emerged from hiding to build a monastery and to construct a new pillar for himself. He was ordained before he returned to living on his pillar. After John died it was said that Simeon became even more minimalist and solitary, eating only what grew on a nearby tree branch. Simeon's visitors received Communion from him by climbing a ladder to reach him. He would even celebrate mass from his platform, and it was said he performed many miracles from it as well. As his life drew to a close, Simeon moved to a new pillar on a more isolated mountainside, where he remained until he died. In all, Simeon lived about seventy years off the ground.

BY GRACIE MORBITZER

The last saint I wanted to write about was Simeon Stylites because there is simply not much about him to which many people can relate. The pillar saints in general just seem so—no pun intended—*unreachable.* I have honestly just never been a fan of hermit saints in the first place. What about the call to community? What good are these saints really doing in the world by separating themselves from it? How can they be doing Jesus's will and helping anyone this way? It is recorded that Simeon was literally trying to avoid other people. Sure, there are many examples of saints who self-isolated to write great works that have in turn helped others grow their faith and daily practices. Sure, he gave advice to a few people, maybe, who were able to afford the journey to visit him and who were physically able to climb a ladder to reach him. Maybe he helped them. But could he not have helped many more who needed his influence on society by living on the ground?

Another problem I have with Simeon and the pillar saints is the fact that not only is living on a pillar isolated but it's also physically challenging. How can we, in this day and age, accept the asceticism of some saints when it in many cases was so extreme that it killed them, quickly putting an end to their beautiful lives and the good they were doing?

In my research I found that even Simeon's contemporaries had some of the same questions. Many people, even those in Church leadership, condemned the actions of the pillar saints, assuming they were self-serving or even performing a publicity stunt. It just rubs me the wrong way to think that much of monastic asceticism arose when Christianity became legal. To me that fact seems to suggest a historical sentiment that if you can't become a saint by being martyred for your faith anymore, you'll have to "martyr yourself" for your faith.

After wrestling with the lives of the pillar saints, I've discovered that my primary question is, Is it unloving to remove oneself from society?

While continually trying to deconstruct the idea that productivity is tantamount to our worth, we also can't deny that Jesus commanded us to use our lives to love one another (while also taking care of ourselves). So, then, don't we need society, and vice versa? Some say that is true only if we, as people, don't belong to ourselves. This gets tricky. The idea of belonging to others is what has perpetuated a history of people abiding abuse, wives being subservient to husbands, and the intense harm done when suicidal folks are called "selfish." While at the same time, belonging only to ourselves suggests we are not connected to all of Creation and one another, which has led to greed, destruction of our earth, and bigotry.

I can't deny that I have certainly felt echoes of these same ideals when I saw, in a similar fashion, friends from Catholic school choose only Catholic colleges and Catholic professions with only Catholic friends—another type of isolation. This phenomenon can apply in any situation where you surround yourself with an ideology and create an echo chamber for your values or ideas. It is nice to have support for your faith and to surround yourself with like-minded people, but by living this way are you also hiding from the "real" world? Are you keeping the gifts of your faith from the people outside of the Church or your peers who need them? It begs the question: are you afraid of your faith being shaken by the influx of new ideas and people who aren't like you?

The flip side of that question is just as challenging—are we required to contribute ourselves to society? Is a person doing what they think is best for themselves also a positive contribution to the community?

I have been looking to modern isolated religious life for answers. They say that in a society that unfortunately still largely uses isolation as punishment, it takes a strong, balanced person to be able to exist on their own. And those living separately are still contributing their prayers, which, they say, are necessary work for the world, too. I believe each of us does need our solitary moments.

Even Jesus needed his. We need our time to learn about peace and slowing down, and to listen. Jesus always returned to society at the end of those periods, but are we all called to do so?

I still can't say I'm a huge fan of St. Simeon Stylites—but he certainly helps us ask a lot of questions. Until we have answers, though, I think I'll stay here, on the ground.

PRAYER

Holy Spirit—guide us in our interactions with others. Help us to be loving, patient, and nonjudgmental. When we are alone, help us to find peace in solitude, and use that time to learn how to listen to God, ourselves, and others. Help us remember to take care of ourselves as best as we can while taking care of one another and our world.

Amen.

ST. MADELEINE SOPHIE BARAT

BORN: **DECEMBER 12, 1779**
DIED: **MAY 25, 1865**
FEAST: **MAY 25**
PATRON OF EDUCATORS, EMBROIDERY, SEWING, PARALYSIS

THE SHORT STORY—Madeleine Sophie grew up in a French peasant family. Her older brother Louis, a seminarian, decided that Sophie needed to be educated and took to teaching her himself, though her level of education was not common for women at the time. Louis went on to become a priest at the height of the French Revolution. He renounced his oath to the revolution and barely escaped execution. When he was released, he brought Sophie with him to Paris. There she learned embroidery and became an excellent seamstress. When she was eighteen years old Sophie discerned that she wanted to enter religious life. She learned the catechism and taught it to children. Louis's superior had a goal to establish a new educational religious society, and he found Madeleine Sophie to be the person for the job. She became part of the Society of the Sacred Heart and began to teach for them in 1801. She founded a second convent and was eventually elected superior general for life. In sixty-three years her group grew to over thirty-five hundred members and it opened more than one hundred schools. Each school was accompanied by a second school designed specifically for impoverished members of the community so that

ARTIST'S STATEMENT—Madeleine Sophie Barat's shirt is embroidered to represent her embroidery trade, and it bears the symbols of her order, the Society of the Sacred Heart. The light hues reflect how I perceive her energy to be—quiet, gentle contemplation. One of my favorite pieces of this icon are the words that show through from the wood's previous life, a perfect nod to Sophie's love of education.

they could have an education as thorough as their peers'. Sophie's wish for every student, especially impoverished young girls, was that they be blessed with a love of learning and have an education like hers.

BY LETICIA OCHOA ADAMS

As of the writing of this book, there are so many disasters happening around the world. We are living with another year of the Covid virus, Russia is still at war with Ukraine, and last year nineteen children were shot in their classroom after their end-of-year awards ceremony. The cost of gas and groceries in the United States is at a forty-year high, and here in Texas, everyone is hot. The heat is not unusual, but when you add it to everything else, it is a tragedy.

I often think that this is the worst moment in my lifetime. I do not remember things ever being this bad in my entire forty-five years of living. Usually, things happen one crisis at a time. I can easily lose perspective and assume that this must be the end times because, I think to myself, *how could it get much worse?* And then I read the lives of the saints.

St. Madeleine Sophie Barat was born in France right before the revolution. It was her experience with the French Revolution that led her to have a heart for justice, centered on the love of God. She saw the importance of leadership that was not harsh and dictatorial; she found ways to resolve conflict, even if that conflict was between reality and ideals. She led the way for women, even those who were nuns, to be in leadership. Her ideas created conflict, but she remained dedicated to them, even in the face of opposition. Her passion was to let people know that they were loved by God.

I knew nothing about St. Madeleine Sophie Barat before being asked to contribute to this project. I randomly picked her name. I ought to know better by now that we do not ever "randomly" pick a saint for anything, they pick us. I have been feeling as if all of this *waves hand around* in the past three years is too much. It is overwhelming, and I'm left wondering where exactly can I, one Hispanic Catholic woman, make a difference?

Reading St. Madeleine Sophie Barat's biography reminded me that these are the times in which saints are made. God calls each of us to sainthood, but these chaotic times are when listening to Him becomes very difficult because there is just so much noise. There are so many opinions on what it means to be a Christ follower and yet, so few people actually doing it. What does it mean to be a Christian? I think we find the answer by looking at the lives of saints like St. Madeleine Sophie Barat, who lived in her own chaotic time and found a way to shine light on the fact that God loves us. She found a way to honor the Sacred Heart of Jesus while creating a group of over three thousand women leaders in the Catholic Church in the 1800s—the same Catholic Church that is currently appalled at the idea of women holding leadership roles. Some things never change, because humans in a fallen world tend to repeat the same patterns, regardless of what history has shown us. It is by remembering the lives of saints like Madeleine Sophie Barat that we can see our way through. Indeed, this might be the craziest time in the history of my life, but it is not the craziest time in all of the history of mankind. It is important for me to gain that perspective.

My favorite line of the Hail Holy Queen is "that we may be made worthy of the promises of Christ." That happens in times like the one we are living in. I used to think being made holy would be comfortable, and boy was I wrong. It is like being burned by a fire whose ashes you rise from. Now, just like revolutionary France, is a time when saints are made in that fire, like St. Madeleine Sophie Barat was.

PRAYER

Dear God, everything is crazy. Everywhere I look there is someone in need. People are tired, angry, and lost. I know how that feels. Please help me to do what it is that you created me to do. To love others the way you love me and to be a witness of your love during so much trauma and pain. Give me the grace to be the kind of leader St. Madeleine Sophie Barat was. Remind me that this life is passing but life with you is eternal. Most of all remind me that everyone on social media is a real person made in your image.

LETICIA OCHOA ADAMS is a Catholic writer and speaker. Her son, Anthony, died by suicide in 2017, and since his death she has focused her work on being a witness to suffering and God's healing. Adams is a contributor to several books, including *Surprised by Life, The Catholic Hipster Handbook, The Ave Prayer Book for Catholic Mothers,* and *Responding to Suicide*. She has a bachelor's degree in philosophy from Holy Apostles College and Seminary. She has written for *Our Sunday Visitor, The National Catholic Reporter, FemCatholic, The Catholic Herald, Patheos,* and *Aleteia*. Adams was a frequent guest on *The Jen Fulwiler Show* on SiriusXM's Catholic Channel and has appeared on a number of podcasts, including *Terrible, Thanks for Asking with Nora McInerny*. She lives with her family in the Austin, Texas, area. You can follow her at Leticiaoadams.com, Facebook: LeticiaOAdamsWriter, Instagram: @leticiaoadams.

STS. SERGIUS AND BACCHUS

ARTIST'S STATEMENT—Sergius and Bacchus understood fear, pain, torture, and humiliation so well. Everyone around them, even old friends, failed to understand them and told them that they were wrong. Today, people still misunderstand Sergius and Bacchus, though for different reasons. I wanted to reflect in this icon the emotions that they felt as a result of their suffering.

BORN: **THIRD CENTURY**

DIED: **~303**

FEAST: **OCTOBER 7**

PATRONS OF SOLDIERS, LGBTQ+ COMMUNITY

THE SHORT STORY—The story goes that Sergius and Bacchus were soldiers in the Roman army, positioned in what is now Syria. They lived as Christians secretly until a day when they avoided entering a Roman temple with the rest of the army and refused to make sacrifices. They were paraded around town in women's clothing, chained together, and publicly humiliated. They were then sentenced to be beaten severely until they would renounce their faith. They would not, and Bacchus died from his injuries. Though Sergius survived, he was subjected to more tortures. The most famous story of the two men describes Bacchus appearing to Sergius the next day as a ghost, encouraging him to keep the faith and reminding him they would at least be together forever in Heaven soon. Sergius was made to wear nails in his shoes, on which he was forced to walk eighteen miles to his execution. He was then beheaded. Historians disagree on the nature of Sergius and Bacchus's relationship, with some suggesting they had entered into a type of early Christian union between men—a blessing ceremony to become "brothers." Though this practice is well documented, its exact nature is still unknown.

BY THEO SWINFORD

I once wondered what the suffering of Christ could possibly have to do with my suffering. It seemed that all anyone around me wanted to do was compare sufferings with Jesus: whatever you're going through, Jesus had it worse, whatever you have suffered, Jesus suffered it first. This kind of thinking was yet another source of shame, yet another reason to think that Christ is far from me. All around me, it seemed, were people who wanted to persuade me that the cross was evidence that Christ understood my experience. But what on earth could the execution of a rabbi in first-century Roman-occupied Judea have to do with the plight of a young Queer in the twenty-first-century United States?

Crucifixion was a humiliating death, and in many ways the ancient Romans perfected it. After being stripped of their clothes and nailed or tied to the cross, victims would slowly suffocate to death before their bodies were left to be eaten by birds, insects, and wild animals. Some accounts of ancient Roman crucifixion report that soldiers entertained themselves by experimenting with new positions in which to crucify their victims, even driving a nail through their genitals.

Many traits of masculinity that still affect our culture can be traced back to ancient Rome. For example, the idea that manliness is rooted in the ability to dominate others. Jesus's movement pushed back against this idea. The English word *virtue* comes from the Latin *vir,* meaning "man"; in other words, to be virtuous was to be manly. Jesus of Nazareth, on the other hand, had a very different idea of what made someone virtuous—and it had nothing to do with dominance. In his view, the truly virtuous were the "meek"—a word that doesn't quite capture the original context. Author and professor Dr. Amy-Jill Levine explains that in Hebrew *meek* described someone who did not lord their power over others. The poor, the meek, the peacemakers, the mourning, the persecuted—these were the blessed, the virtuous, the worthy.

When Sergius and Bacchus were discovered to be Christians, the Romans dressed them as women because in the eyes of their abusers this was a humiliating and degrading state for men to be in. That same prejudice infects the hearts of many today and causes the deaths of my trans siblings, especially trans women of color. This story shows me that Christ's suffering has everything to do with my suffering—and the suffering of Queer people everywhere. We are not excluded from redemption even when others make us feel excluded. Christ himself and the saints know the humiliation, the abuse, and the trauma that we've been through, living in a world that promises power to those who make us feel powerless. But Christ, instead, promises us that the Almighty is on the side of the lowly, ignored, and outcast.

With that promise in my heart, I cry out with the saints for mercy. For every transgender person who has been murdered. For every LGBTQ+ person who has been harassed on the street. For every Queer person who lives in fear all around the world. For every young person who has died from homophobic and transphobic violence, whether that violence be physical, verbal, or emotional. Sergius and Bacchus have been a beacon of hope for centuries for their unwavering belief that God loves them when no one else does, for their defiance when the Romans tried to shame them into betraying God and themselves. This, I believe, is the charism of the Queer community, that despite all of the abuse and the violence, we rise up and claim that we are Beloved.

PRAYER

Sts. Sergius and Bacchus, pray with us.

Holy Trinity, Creator and Liberator, we ask for your protection on those who live in fear or shame. We ask your protection on the LGBTQ+ community, especially those who are young, homeless, or forgotten. We thank you for the gift of our unique identities, and we ask you to grant us the grace of celebrating ourselves in all that You created us to be. Holy Spirit, come upon us and send us out to share this joy with all who need healing. Amen.

THEO SWINFORD (they/them) is a theologian, writer, and teacher. They completed their BA in theology and religious studies at St. Mary's University in London. They live in Brooklyn with their partner.

ST. KEVIN

BORN: **498**

DIED: **618**

FEAST: **JUNE 3**

PATRON OF BLACKBIRDS, IRELAND, SINGLE MEN, LIVESTOCK

THE SHORT STORY—At an early age Kevin chose to enter into religious life and left home to become a hermit. He had already attracted many followers inspired by his faith, and he made this move largely to find solitude and seclusion. For seven years Kevin spent his time in prayer and lived with only the birds and other animals, sleeping on, eating, and wearing only what nature provided for him. This move itself was attractive to even more followers, however, and they built a small community close to Kevin's cave. He soon developed this community into a monastery and seminary. After a pilgrimage to Rome, Kevin spent another four years in solitude before returning to his monks at Glendalough. Under his leadership, it became the most influential, thriving monastic community in Ireland.

BY TRACY BALZER

High in the Wicklow Mountains of Ireland stand some of the best-preserved ruins of ancient Celtic monasticism. The name Glendalough (pronounced with a hard *k* at the end) means "valley of two lakes" in Irish Gaelic. One can hardly imagine a more idyllic place to establish a community of prayer and learning, surrounded

ARTIST'S STATEMENT—Kevin sits deep in meditation. The color palette in this icon comes from the region he chose and loved, and the bird from his story sits on one shoulder—nest on the other, as he waits patiently.

by the verdant green flora that is so quintessentially Irish, and craggy mountains that speak of God's protective presence.

I have visited Glendalough several times, because it is quite accessible by tour bus from Dublin. As I have walked among its stony ruins, entering through an arched stone gateway, past the impressive stone tower, and on to St. Kevin's church, it is impossible to ignore the sanctity of the place. So many prayers were prayed here, so many lives dedicated to God here. So much natural beauty exists here. It is a "thin place" indeed, where the line between earth and Heaven seems tissue-paper thin.

St. Kevin is now hailed as one of Ireland's great Celtic saints. Yet tradition claims that the glory that was (and is) Glendalough did not initially feature in Kevin's vision, certainly not at the magnitude that eventually classified it as a "monastic city." It is believed that Kevin initially set out to live a prayerful life of solitude and chose Glendalough as his hermitage. The foundations of his cell remain today. But eventually, despite Kevin's original plan, his reputation as a holy man spread regardless. Seekers came to him, persuading him to teach and lead them in their spiritual formation. So Kevin gave up his vision of a solitary life, and he accepted the call to pastoral leadership of a Christian community.

Like the stories of so many great Celtic saints, Kevin's story is peppered with legends that celebrate his sanctity. One of the most famous and most whimsical involves the hermit himself and a family of birds.

The tale is told of the time Kevin lay on his back on the floor of his hermitage, arms stretched to each side—the cruciform posture that saints through the ages have adopted when in prayer. So concentrated was Kevin's contemplation that he did not notice that a bird had built its nest in one of his open hands and proceeded to lay its eggs there. Kevin, being especially keen to honor all of God's creation, refused to rise from his floor. The story goes that he lay there, praying and waiting, day after day until the eggs hatched and the fledglings finally abandoned their nest in the hermitage.

This is a charming story, a winsome story. A story of selflessness and compassion, and of the relinquishment of one's own agenda for God's. I have often pondered this story as a parable that encourages me to be more like Kevin—more patient and selfless. It reminds me that I am too possessive of my own agenda for my life; that perhaps God wants to use me to help bring about new life somewhere or for someone, and I need just to "lie still." I think this is not at all a bad way to apply Kevin's story to my modern-day life.

But more recently I've considered a different angle. In addition to trying to learn from the patient and prayerful Kevin, I've come to see myself as occupying one of those tiny blue eggs. (It's not known what species of bird may have built this nest, but birds' eggs are always a lovely robin's-egg blue in my mind.) In this version, Jesus himself is in Kevin's place, lying in the position of the cross and sacrificially, prayerfully holding me in his care while I slowly grow into the creature he has made me to be.

There is no better place for me to be than in the nurturing hand of the Lord. In his protective care a "hatching" will result, and new life will emerge in me.

And I will fly.

PRAYER

How lovely is your dwelling place,
Lord Almighty . . .
Even the sparrow has found a home,
and the swallow a nest for herself,
where she may have her young—
a place near your altar,
*Lord Almighty, my King and my God.**

Thank you, Lord, that you hold me in the palm of your hand,
and that you are doing a new and good work in me.
Amen.

* From Psalm 84 (NIV).

TRACY BALZER is an author, campus minister, professor, and spiritual director with a passion for Celtic and contemplative spirituality. She leads spiritual retreats to the Isle of Iona, Scotland, annually. Her newest book is *A Journey of Sea and Stone: How Holy Places Guide and Renew Us* (Broadleaf). Tracy is married to Cary, and they live in Siloam Springs, Arkansas.

ARTIST'S STATEMENT—Although he bears some scars and an exhausted expression from his tireless work and travels, I still wanted St. Paul in this icon to have a gleam in his eye, representing the mission that was more important to him than his life and free-

BORN: **~5**

DIED: **~64–67**

FEAST: **JUNE 29**

PATRON OF MISSIONS, THEOLOGIANS, WRITERS, CAMPING, EQUESTRIANS

THE SHORT STORY—The only thing we know of Paul's early life is that he actively engaged in persecuting, torturing, and arresting Christians. He played a part in the martyrdom of St. Stephen among others. Paul was traveling when he had a vision of Jesus that was so bright it blinded him. He heard Jesus's voice asking him why he was persecuting him. Paul was led for three days in his blindness as he fasted and spent time in prayer until a man named Ananias was sent to restore his sight and baptize him. Paul then set out on his mission to travel the world and tell as many people as he could about Jesus. He took three journeys, on the first of which St. Barnabas accompanied him, through Cyprus and Asia Minor, where they established Churches. Paul kept up with these communities through letters, in which he gave advice and answered questions. He continued to travel through much of what is now Europe, despite resistance from his own Jewish people and the antagonism of the Roman authorities, who imprisoned him for his outspokenness. During Paul's journeys he suffered shipwrecks, beatings, communities turning on him, opposition to his ideas by other Apostles, companions deserting him, churches preaching differing ideas, riots, and attacks on his life. Finally, in Rome between the years 63 and 67, Paul was arrested and put on trial a final time. Early documents and Church writings agree that he was martyred, but the method is unknown, with most suggesting he was beheaded.

BY RYAN J. PELTON

I resonate with St. Paul. Not because I wrote most of the New Testament, or have made any great contribution to the two-thousand-year-old movement that's still growing under the influence of this great saint. I resonate with Saul from Tarsus because of his reluctance.

My work as a pastor in the twenty-first century is nothing on the level of St. Paul's. But the reluctance of the Apostle "untimely born" rattles around in my soul, too. Paul went from being a well-educated and well-read Pharisee bent on wiping out early disciples of Jesus to being a follower of the Messiah, and one of the Christian movement's most fruitful ambassadors. The kinship I feel toward Saul (later called Paul) is because of his hesitancy around calling: "For I am the least of the apostles, unworthy to be called an apostle, because I persecuted the church of God" (1 Corinthians 15:9 ESV).

Least, unworthy, and an honest admission of violence are words of reluctance. They are not confident words from a man who endured prison, snakebites, and near-death experiences for the message of grace. I resonate with St. Paul because unworthiness is often a nagging cold I carry around despite warmer weather on the horizon.

My leastness and unworthiness and reluctance take on many shapes. Unworthiness for not living up to the standards of faith, hope, and love. Instead of having faith in God for his provision, I take matters into my own hands. Instead of having hope in the promise of resurrection, I live with anxiety and fear of tomorrow. And instead of having love, I choose indifference to God and neighbor.

The reluctance and unworthiness I experience can also take the form of false narratives of success: a big church, book deals for expertise in particular theological ideas, and invitations to the conferences that prop up the church-industrial complex. I sometimes wonder if Paul experienced the same unworthiness, leastness, and reluctance I feel when I'm around other pastors who seem more successful.

My resonance with Paul and his reluctance in Gospel ministry is not because I pastor a smaller church. My reluctance comes from my past, much like Paul's admission of sin and violence against the Church. I've always felt like an outsider and worried that one day the Church police would come and revoke my pastor's card. My call to Jesus, and to ministry, was much like St. Paul's Damascus Road experience. I didn't have the same foundation in the Hebrew Scriptures, but I was running away from Jesus, and running fast. I found myself in a pit of drinking, drugs, and unhealthy relationships. The only suitable rescue would require Divine help. Fortunately, Jesus called, and I was ready to listen.

Paul was not a fan of Christians and wanted them wiped off the face of the earth. My taste for the Jesus-tribe was bitter and I thought most Jesus freaks came off as hypocritical. I've since become more patient and understand that, like in the story of the Prodigal Son, both the younger and older brothers need grace.

I connect to Paul's reluctance as a Christian and a pastor—Paul's past often haunting his present. And yet the saint from Tarsus never dodged the hard parts of his past. When the scales lifted from Paul's eyes, he saw the world through the Technicolor lens of grace. His life—past, present, future—and his calling: all grace.

When St. Paul considered his past achievements, they were nothing compared to knowing the Messiah. He said, "I count everything as loss" (Philippians 3:8 ESV). Grace, grace. When Paul dealt with a "thorn in [his] side" (2 Corinthians 12:7 ESV), which some suggest was a physical disability, he celebrated his weakness, and he leaned into "sufficient grace" (2 Corinthians 12:9 ESV). When Paul greeted the churches he planted around the Roman Empire, despite their unfaithfulness, division, and problems, he began with "grace and peace to you" (Romans 1:7 ESV). And one of Paul's most stunning confessions: after dealing with his past, his calling, and his reluctance, he says, "But by the grace of God I am what I am, and his grace toward me was not in vain" (1 Corinthians 15:10 ESV).

I resonate with St. Paul because despite his own leastness, unworthiness, his past, and reluctance as a follower of Jesus, and an Apostle, something greater than himself, beyond our imaginations, an indescribable gift, took hold: the gift of grace.

PRAYER

Father, we thank you for St. Paul, who reminds us that unworthiness and reluctance don't have the final word. We thank you that despite our sins and failures, grace wins. We thank you despite our fears, anxieties, doubts, and worries about the past. You have good works for us to do in the future. Lord, help us marvel at your grace, help us live by grace, and help us share your grace with others.

Amen.

RYAN J. PELTON (MA, Calvin Theological Seminary) is Lead Pastor of New City Church, where he leads, teaches, preaches, and helps plant churches in Kansas City, Missouri, and beyond. Ryan has planted several churches, served in pastoral ministry, and authored multiple nonfiction and fiction books for the last twenty-two years. He and his wife, Christy, and their four children live in Kansas City. They enjoy the outdoors, watching sports, good food, good company, and exploring the city they call home.

JOHN THE
PTIST

TATEMENT—I kept within the tradition of portraying John as very thin, shirt-
h lots of hair—which are all details depicted in traditional icons of him. He
nd shell (symbolizing baptism) tattoos, and his neck is mostly obscured,
the type of death he is associated with. His expression is downcast, but he
ead high, representing the pride he still had throughout the tough life he

BORN: **LATE FIRST CENTURY B.C.**

DIED: **~28–36**

FEAST: **JUNE 24**

PATRON OF JORDAN, PUERTO RICO, BAPTISM, RIVERS, MESSENGERS

THE SHORT STORY—John was the cousin of Jesus who famously leapt within the womb of his mother, Elizabeth, when Mary, pregnant with Jesus, visited her. He spent his adult life in the desert eating nothing but wild honey and locusts and wearing animal skins, baptizing people, and proclaiming the coming Messiah. He recognized Jesus as that Messiah when Jesus came to him to be baptized. He was later imprisoned for speaking out against the king's illegal divorce and remarriage. He was killed when the king promised his stepdaughter any gift and her mother persuaded her to ask for John's head.

BY BOND STRONG

As a child I was captivated by the endearing story of how John the Baptist leapt in his mother's womb at the sound of Mary's greeting. The story has everything a sweet, appropriate, child-friendly story should: kind greetings, obedience, familial love, and acceptance. It is a holy story but, without the context of the rest of the characters, utterly tame. It is still one of my favorite stories in Scripture, and I love meditating on it while praying the rosary—mostly because it points to the future of both of those precious babies, a future where one would enthusiastically prepare the way for the other to save him. As an innocent baby, John fit sweetly into the nativity story, but as an adult he evolved into a challenging, even dangerous figure, reflecting the life of the one he prepared for. He too died a painful and unjust death. The only thing neat and proper about John the Baptist—a radical social, religious, and political figure—was the context in which I usually heard of him, namely, Sunday school.

As I grew up and stretched my spiritual muscles, I encountered John in other ways and traditions. In charismatic circles his mystical status as prophet and forerunner was emphasized. In the Baptist Church, his evangelistic efforts were highlighted along with his perceived connection to believers' baptism. Eventually I found my way into the Catholic Church, where I discovered him as a saint.

Discovering John the Baptist as a saint prompted me to look more deeply into his life. I was amazed by how much Scripture is devoted to him and also how unacceptable he was in so many ways. The active, delighted baby grew up to be a serious person who played an integral role in the life of Jesus. He baptized Jesus, and he called him family.

It must have been extremely difficult for John to live on the fringes of society—in the desert wilderness, holding on to the spiritual knowledge he had been gifted, and sharing it with people, some of whom rejected it. Eating locusts and honey, and wearing unconventional clothing were outward and visible signs of his interior spiritual radicalism. In fewer words: John was weird and mysterious, and he was also truthful, passionate, and unwaveringly devoted to his calling from God.

If he was worried about what others thought of his unconventional life and ministry, Scripture doesn't mention it. We are given a portrait of a man fearless in his delivery of the message God had given him: repent. It is as popular a message today as it was then, but people still came, and listened, and were baptized. They listened for the same reason that we listen to figures like Servant of God Dorothy Day and St. Teresa of Calcutta and that we don't listen to the preacher on the side of the street announcing nothing but hellfire and brimstone or the swanky televangelist: authenticity. People like John knew the work God set before them and they did it. They gave their minds, souls, and bodies to Jesus, and nothing about their lives looked like any that had been lived before.

In my mind and in my heart, John the Baptist calls me to a radical acceptance of the person God has made me to be and the work he has given me to do, even if it challenges what is socially acceptable. In fact, following God authentically always challenges convention—even religious convention.

John is everything I love about being a Christian and a Catholic. He embodies the subversiveness I adore about Christ and his Church. He is an example of the authenticity that can still assert itself amid the politics, disunity, and distraction in the Church. John was and is present with those on the margins and peripheries, just as Jesus calls me to be. Those of us who eat, dress, and think differently than culture dictates have a place in this Church and an important role to play in this world. By the manner of his death, John shows me there is a cost to authenticity, but his willingness speaks to the hope he had in what his Lord would accomplish in his death and resurrection. He is still preparing the way for me to receive Jesus authentically. And he is calling me to prepare the way for those who would tread through this wilderness in search of Jesus our Lord.

PRAYER

Lord, help us to live authentically. Help us to accept who you made each one of us to be, so we can fulfill the purpose you have given us. Reveal to us how you are preparing us in the wilderness so we can prepare the way for others. Thank you for our baptism; help us to sincerely repent.

St. John the Baptist, who leapt with joy at the sound of Mary's voice, and who faithfully and reverently baptized our Lord, pray for us!

BOND STRONG lives in the mountains of southwest Virginia with her husband, two sons, and cat. She works as a pilgrimage group coordinator, attempts to read fifty books every year, and is particularly passionate about ecumenical discussions between Christian traditions.

ST. JUAN DIEGO

ARTIST'S STATEMENT—Juan Diego had quite a lot to process at once—and I wanted his face to show that. He had no idea what was about to happen. He holds the roses in his shirt right after realizing the image of Mary is imprinted on it. With this saint in particular, I wanted the clothing to be as representative of everyday, casual wear as possible.

BORN: **1474**

DIED: **1548**

FEAST: **DECEMBER 9**

PATRON OF INDIGENOUS PEOPLE

THE SHORT STORY—Juan Diego was born in 1474, in what is now Mexico City. His given name was Cuauhtlatoatzin, which means "talking eagle." His father died when Juan Diego was young, so he went to live with his uncle. Juan was a very spiritual man in the Aztec religion, but when Franciscan missionaries arrived, he and his wife were among the very first group to be baptized Catholic. He was very devoted to the faith, often traveling as far as he needed to learn more about it. One morning while he was on his way (in a hurry) to mass on the outskirts of the city, a radiant woman stopped him. She told Juan that she was not only the mother of Jesus but also the mother of all who lived in this land. She asked him to build a chapel for her on the hill, to serve as a place of peace for the distressed. Juan took this request to the bishop, who did not believe him. When he encountered Mary again, Juan told her that perhaps she needed to ask someone else to complete this mission—he did not think he was either worthy or capable enough. She refused, though, saying she wanted only him to carry out her request. The next day, when Juan's uncle fell very ill, he was distraught over the situation. However, Mary appeared to him again and asked, "Am I not here, I who am your mother?" She told him that his uncle had already recovered while he was out, and she asked him to climb the hill and gather flowers in his cloak. She blessed them and told him to bring them to the bishop. When he arrived, he poured out the flowers and found the image of Mary on the cloak. He returned to his uncle the next day and found that he was indeed cured. Juan Diego lived out the rest of his life on the hill, caring for the church and the people who made pilgrimages there.

BY KARLA MENDOZA ARANA

At eleven years old I was waiting at the airport to get on a plane that would take me from Lima, Peru, to an unknown city in the United States of America. I didn't even think about where I was going because the only thing I knew was that after one year of being apart, I was finally going to reunite with my papi.

On my side of the globe the early days of summer were starting to bloom, yet I wore a wool peacoat that my papi's oldest sister, my tía Olga, had given to me. The moment my mami, my sister, and I landed in Chicago for a layover I understood that my little fashion coat was made for Lima winters but not for the cold winters of the U.S. Midwest. Within weeks of moving to the United States we went to a secondhand store where I chose a light blue coat, and just like that, I had to put the gift from my tía away in the closet.

I could not have expected putting my coat away in the closet would foreshadow my future experience. Moving to a new country when you're eleven years old is no easy feat. I was young enough to still be a kid but old enough to remember my family and cultural traditions, the smell of the Pacific Ocean every morning on my way to school, and all the friendships that meant the world to me. I quietly stored those memories in the pockets of my coat, hoping to keep them safe there.

The quickest way to survive in a place is to assimilate, and while I didn't have the words then to communicate what was happening, I know now that's what I was doing. I learned a new language, new cultures, new traditions, new histories, new foods, and new landscapes while putting away my own.

Yet God doesn't forget who we really are, God remembers our true name.

That the Lord knows our names is what strikes me about the

story of Juan Diego. He was a humble man, one of the first in his Indigenous community to be baptized. He was walking to mass when he heard someone calling his name.

He heard a voice: "Cuauhtlatoazin." Maybe he looked around wondering who was also running late to mass. She called him again: "Cuauhtlatoazin." And that's when he saw her, the dark-skinned Mother of Jesus. And she revealed her own name, Guadalupe.

I believe imagination and wonder lead to faith, so in my imagination I wonder if the reason she called him by his name was to acknowledge the power and courage he carried in his name. After all, Cuauhtlatoazin means "talking eagle" or "the one who speaks with authority." In the moment when he chose to receive the blessing of being called by his name, he changed history. Not just for himself but for an entire country, and for the Catholic Church.

Perhaps it was the confidence of knowing his name that made Juan Diego walk up the hill in the middle of winter to look for flowers. When I read how he hid them in his cloak, I am reminded of my own flowers hidden in a coat pocket in a dark closet where no one can see them. Juan Diego took the risk and showed his flowers to the bishop, letting him know the power Juan Diego found through his divine encounters, his own faith, and his own name. Imagine the surprise when the flowers fell and made up the image of the beloved Virgen de Guadalupe.*

I remember the day when I quietly and secretly walked up a hill in the middle of winter, hoping to find the flowers I had long ago lost to assimilation and to survival. The wilderness often feels like winter with no flowers left to bloom. To my surprise, when I took the risk of looking back, I found the flowers had never stopped blooming, they were just waiting to be found again. Even after all those years of assimilation, of hiding my real name, I found God and She welcomed me with Love.

Juan Diego lived the rest of his life welcoming and loving every-

* "Our Lady of Guadalupe" in Spanish.

one who came to the chapel to find peace and grace there, yet I wonder how many times he could still hear the voice of La Morenita† calling his name.

PRAYER

God who remembers our names,

Whether they are names that we chose for ourselves, or names given to us in love, thank you for reminding us that it's never too late to reconnect to our people, our traditions, our cultures as we seek to love you and love others the way you love them. God who meets us in the middle of winter, in the wilderness, thank you for reminding us that life can still be found here. May we too hear the call of Love as we walk up the hill.

Amen.

KARLA MENDOZA ARANA was born in Lima, Peru, where the Pacific Ocean was her best friend. She migrated to the United States with her mom and sister when she was eleven years old to reunite with her dad in the land of the Anishinaabe in the Midwest. She has spent the last few years healing and reclaiming her story after many years of assimilating to whiteness. She sits at the intersections of being a Jesus-loving Afro-Indigenous Peruvian woman, a fat woman, and one who has experienced the United States as an undocumented citizen. She dabbles in storytelling, visual arts, writing, teaching, bookbinding, photography, and podcasting. Most of all, Karla loves laughter, the color yellow, dancing to Bad Bunny, single-origin pourovers, and reading multiple books at once.

† La Morenita is the endearing name given to Our Lady of Guadalupe. The literal translation is "the little dark-skinned one."

Maria
Zenia

BORN: **1831**

DIED: **1877**

FEAST: **JULY 12**

PATRON OF MARRIED COUPLES, FAMILIES, BREAST CANCER, ENTREPRENEURS AND SMALL BUSINESSES, FAMILY BUSINESSES, WORKING PARENTS

THE SHORT STORY—Zélie tried to enter the religious life when she was young, but she was turned away because of her poor health. She took up lacework and soon had her own small business. She met her husband, Louis, in 1858 and the two had nine children, with four dying in infancy. Louis soon sold his watchmaking business and became a partner in Zélie's lace business because she had become so successful. The family spent much time in nature, cared for their parents as they aged, and made a few pilgrimages to holy sites. When their youngest daughter, Thérèse, was only four, Zélie died from breast cancer. Thérèse later became a saint and Doctor of the Church, and Louis and Zélie were the first married couple canonized together.

BY CLAIRE SWINARSKI

To be a mother is to be a worker.

Those of us with children know this. I can get in ten thousand steps per day just chasing after my three little ones. There's always someone to be fed, someone who needs a Band-Aid, someone who was given juice in the wrong color cup. There are tears to

ARTIST'S STATEMENT—Zélie's craft and livelihood—lace—is featured prominently in her clothing. In this icon she looks up to the light and smiles despite messy hair and a tired face.

wipe, tantrums to soothe, and books to read. It is a never-ending labor, one where you don't clock out and can't hide in the break room. Some women—including myself—run not only our households but our own businesses. On days when I want to crawl under a blanket and sleep for seven solid weeks, I gain strength to carry on from inspiring saints like St. Zélie Martin.

St. Zélie was a mother to nine, including five daughters who reached adulthood and all had religious vocations. She was also a lacemaker and became well known for her artistic talents and keen business mind. She also raised a Doctor of the Church, her daughter Thérèse, before succumbing to breast cancer in 1877.

Zélie, best known as the mother of St. Thérèse of Lisieux, often has this saying attributed to her: "It's necessary that the heroic become daily and that the daily become heroic." Those small, seemingly insignificant acts of brushing her daughters' hair or paying her employees? She saw in them the larger picture. Her paychecks reminded her lacemakers of their inherent dignity. Making dinner for her family filled them not just with sustenance but with the knowledge that they were loved, which is the most precious stone a person could possibly carry. Her everyday work was not insignificant; it was the way she expressed love and faithfulness to her family and the world at large.

In today's world, we're often presented with a false dichotomous choice.

Raise your children well *or* provide for their needs financially.

Be the parent who drops them off at school *or* pursue your creative interests.

Put your kids first *or* use your mind in interesting, beneficial ways.

In other words, be a mother *or* a worker, as if motherhood isn't work in its purest form: a selfless labor that flows from love.

St. Zélie inspires me to raise both saints and money. To offer my God-given gifts and talents to those who would benefit from them, inside my house and outside of it. To manage a household and employees, to thrive as mother and as worker.

Reading Proverbs 31 sometimes tempts me to roll my eyes. Being the perfect wife? Not exactly on my to-do list. But when I read it through the eyes of St. Zélie, a new picture emerges—one of a strong, fearless woman whose lamp doesn't go out at night, whose children rise and call her blessed. Not only can I be a good mother and a good businesswoman but I am called to . . . be. And if being faithful to the call of God means angering people who've drawn moral lines in the sand where there are none, well, take it up with the Lord.

Above all else, St. Zélie inspires me to love. She reminds me of the importance of loving my family, and of pouring love into the work that I do. Women running businesses aren't anything new or novel. However, doing so today is just as difficult, uncomfortable, and complicated as it was in Zélie's time. The balancing act is just as tricky. But St. Zélie consistently ordered her life around a love of God, and she inspires me to do the same.

Because my foundation is built on Christ. Not on age-old gender roles or modern, secular dictations. Not on political theories or socialized desires.

On he who loves, and is love himself.

PRAYER

St. Zélie, show those of us who fill the roles of parents—especially mothers—how necessary and holy our work is. Bring us the joy that comes with the love of others and the rest we need to be able to continue. Allow us to fulfill all of our greatest desires both within and outside of our families. Amen.

CLAIRE SWINARSKI is the author of multiple books for both adults and children, as well as the founder of *The Catholic Feminist*. She lives in small-town Wisconsin with her family.

ST. CHRISTOPHER

ARTIST'S STATEMENT—In this icon, I made Christopher resemble an experienced hiker on the move—not only a large man but also a humble one in pursuit of knowledge and greatness. With his staff (walking stick) and travel pack strap bearing patches from all of the places he's been, he's on a mission and seeing the world, all in the name of the

BORN: **~200**

DIED: **251**

FEAST: **JULY 25**

PATRON OF TRANSPORTATION, TRAVEL, UNMARRIED MEN, STORMS, EPILEPSY, SURFING, MOUNTAINEERING

THE SHORT STORY—Christopher decided he wanted to serve only the greatest person in existence—he journeyed around the world and searched until he decided he had found that it was someone named Jesus. After learning about Christianity from a monk and studying to live like the monks did, Christopher found that he could serve Jesus much better by applying his own talents for good. He did this by using his size and strength to carry people across a dangerous river until one day he carried a child who grew so heavy in his arms they almost didn't make it. On the other side, the child said he was Jesus and that Christopher had carried the weight of the world, and then the child disappeared. Christopher spent the rest of his life traveling, preaching, and using his life for good.

BY GRACIE MORBITZER

Okay, so maybe you know you're not a leader, or a speaker or writer, or a visual artist. Maybe you're not great at making anything. Maybe you're shy or socially anxious. Maybe you really just can't think of how you're going to use your gifts for your faith like the saints have.

Well, I hope Christopher can help you figure it out.

I like to believe, since we don't have much information about him, that he honestly was not good at anything. His job before he began to travel was being a servant for a king, so maybe he wasn't coordinated enough to do any other palace chores. We learn about Christopher following a band of thieves for a while because he was convinced their leader was the greatest person in existence, but he didn't stick around long. Not only was Christopher likely onto a new lead but I bet he wasn't very good at their thieving work either. Then we learn about how a monk taught him to fast and pray, but Christopher wasn't very good at those things either. Not even prayer? Yes—one of the most basic practices of faith. And yet he was still faithful, still loved Jesus, and wanted to do good. The monk suggested that Christopher use something he did have—his physical attributes—to do something that would help people—and this suggestion stuck. Christopher found motivation and purpose in this task, which likely no one else could have performed. He began to carry people, even grown adults, across a river that was so violent people were known to drown while trying to cross it.

And Christopher offered up this task, which probably was exhausting and dangerous, to Jesus. We learn later that he's rewarded for it by meeting Christ. But even if he hadn't met Christ, Christopher's story would have been one of success. Anytime someone finds a purpose, a faith, and a life that is satisfying and fulfilling, it is a success; and that's what Christopher did.

The second part of his story involves his patronage: travel.

There are a few other patron saints of travel, but Christopher is the most popular, and the one whose medal we keep in our cars. We don't know how far he journeyed, or for how long, but we do know he spent the beginning and the end of his life traveling, first pursuing truth, and then trying to spread it.

I can't help but think that the miracle of Christopher carrying the child Jesus was just God's way of telling him that he wanted him to keep going, to get out there in the world again.

Real travel—the kind that doesn't aim to conquer, claim land or objects, or insert oneself forcibly and disrespectfully into another place—really is God-like. The kind that simply aims to be somewhere—see it, understand it, live and learn what it can teach you, is holy. It allows you to empathize with and understand people unlike yourself. It inspires. It fills your soul with wonder and awe. It reminds you of your impermanence and smallness by removing you from a set routine, and it challenges your ideas and perceptions. It breaks down hate by breaking down fear of difference, and it allows respect to grow instead. It is nearly essential to break out of your miniscule square inch of the world to better understand God and humanity and love and life.

Christopher would be telling you this if he were around today. He'd be standing at the entrance to the Appalachian Trail, hiking poles in hand and gigantic backpack on, keeping everyone's spirits up along the length of the journey as he sings, jokes, helps people over obstacles, and shares extras of everything packed for when someone runs out. In short he'd be helping people through their emotional and spiritual journeys. He'd be the one at the visitors' center or travel agency that has such a spark when he talks about a place that you itch to go see it yourself. He'd be the guy who doesn't even own a house—just a van—and is always sending his friends postcards from the places he stops. He'd be visiting not only churches and holy sites but also natural wonders and parks and every place of cultural importance to discover what he can learn and absorb from them. He'd be taking chances on cuisine, where trails end, and games or crafts, and loving every minute, even if he isn't good at much, if any of it.

PRAYER

To travel through this world and this life is dangerous. There is so much unknown, so many challenges, and so many choices. St. Christopher, like you, may we bear each challenge for and with Jesus, and may we never be afraid of the unseen road ahead. Keep us safe on our journeys, and show us all the lessons and amazing wonders to be seen.

Amen.

ST. ANNE

BORN: **FIRST CENTURY B.C.**

DIED: **FIRST CENTURY B.C. OR A.D.**

FEAST: **JULY 26**

PATRON OF GRANDPARENTS, WOMEN IN LABOR, CHILDLESSNESS, AND INFERTILITY

THE SHORT STORY—St. Anne and her husband, St. Joachim, are traditionally regarded as the parents of Mary and the grandparents of Jesus. The only stories we have of them are from a noncanonical document called "The Gospel of James." It says that the two were childless, and Joachim went to the temple to offer a holiday sacrifice. While there he was ridiculed for not having any children and was not allowed to enter and present his offering. Joachim was also told that he was unworthy. Devastated, he fled to the mountains to pray and beg God for children. Anne learned what had happened to her husband, and she made a promise to God that if she were allowed to have a child, she would dedicate them to God. At the same moment, both Anne and Joachim had a vision of an angel who told them Anne would bear a "wondrous" child. Most legends indicate that Joachim may have died shortly after the birth of Mary.

ARTIST'S STATEMENT—Luckily, people are beginning to share their stories of infertility. Because it was too taboo to discuss until not very long ago (and is still not considered safe in some places), we are finally realizing how common infertility is—and how traumatic. Hearing about St. Anne—the very mother of the mother of God—struggling with this same issue is so humanizing of her. That trauma is something I wanted very visible on her face, along with worry—as on the face of any mother—especially one with a child and grandchild about to change the world.

BY ERIN S. LANE

When my ten-year-old daughter got her first period, I threw her a party. I threw her multiple parties, actually. I wanted her to know that menarche wasn't just some shrink-wrapped secret to tuck away in tiny purses and back pockets but something to celebrate. But what exactly to celebrate about this aspect of womanhood—of being human—and how to name it? As a feminist theologian prone to overthinking, I was not so sure.

The first period party was small, at a park, with watermelon, hot fries, and a bottle of sparkling apple juice from a Mexican tienda. *"Algo roso"*—something red—I'd texted my daughter's birth mother when she'd asked what to bring. Food had always been a reliable way for us to convey what words could not. While fuchsia flesh dripped down my chin, and my daughter chased sisters in the distance, her mother leaned over the picnic table and asked, "She not too young?" "No, not too young." I shook my head and smiled wide. *"Es bueno."* Bodies are good.

But ten did feel too young to be celebrating this child—any child—"becoming a woman," which still seemed the most common way of framing the onset of menstruation and possibility of pregnancy. It was that last bit I found unsettling. Why did the entry into womanhood have to hinge on one's fitness for motherhood? What about biologically childfree women like myself? Were we lesser women if we didn't want our period, didn't need our period, to make family? What about women who didn't get their periods—whether because of anatomy, hysterectomy, or the gradual tides of aging? Were they any less worthy of awe and belonging? What about women for whom their periods were regular reminders that they were not mothers, not this time, not this way, that they were not woman enough?

I don't know if St. Anne got her period every month. If its absence was a symptom of her infertility. Or if its arrival brought a quiet suffering. (And, sometimes, relief?) We know from one of the apocryphal texts, "The Infancy Gospel of James," that she and Joachim grieved their childlessness. But whether this was because of its stigma or its reality is never stated. When Joachim brings his gift to the temple, he's censured for his lack of seed and not allowed to go first in the ritual offering. When Anne mourns the couple's misfortune, she mourns not a personal desire for motherhood but the reproach of her religious community. Crying out to God, she laments how she has "become a curse before the children of Israel" and how they've "mocked me forth out of the temple of the Lord" (3:1, M. R. James translation).

Like many of the barren biblical matriarchs before her, Anne is granted her prayer for a child: Mary, eventual mother of Jesus. I suppose, by accounts both traditional and modern, this is a happy ending. It is certainly hard for me to imagine the course of human history without the arrival of Mary, though the God I know has a habit of finding a way where there is no way. But I wonder if the happy ending is not that a child gives your life meaning but that your longing gives life meaning. I wonder if the happy ending is not that a family makes you blessed but that your honesty is a blessing. I wonder if the happy ending is not that Anne is now "woman enough" but that she was already enough to sit at Heaven's feet. "Woe unto me, unto what I am likened?" she pleads (3:2, M. R. James translation), and I imagine God responding, "Unto what are you likened? Woman, you are like me."

My daughter's second period party was bigger, at our home, with fruit salad, rose petals, and sanitary pads for name tags. The guests were an eclectic bunch—a conservative mom from church, a witchy friend from way back. While my husband served pancakes—we needn't keep shrink-wrapped secrets from men either—we went around the table and spoke words of gratitude. What we liked about being women. What we liked about my daughter being among us. We ended by each reading a blessing. I read Lucille Clifton's "Poem in Praise of Menstruation." I told my daughter she was a powerful river, "beautiful and faithful and ancient / and female and brave."

My daughter's birthday falls on St. Anne's feast day. I've never celebrated the latter, but this year I might. This year, I just might know what to celebrate, what to pray:

PRAYER

God of Rivers Red and Rocky: You have made each of us beautiful and faithful and ancient and human *and brave. May we never forget our body's wild and wondrous power and the source of its ever-flowing enoughness in you. That alone is worth a party. Period.*

ERIN S. LANE is the author of *Someone Other Than a Mother: Flipping the Scripts on a Woman's Purpose and Making Meaning Beyond Mothering.* She lives in Raleigh, North Carolina, with her improbable kin. Follow her work at www.erinslane.com or on social media @heyerinlane.

ST. MARTHA

ARTIST'S STATEMENT—In this icon Martha holds a spoon as a symbol of her patronage of cooks, and in reference to the story of her preparations while Jesus visited. Her apron bears the symbol of a dragon, which she was said by noncanonical stories to have tamed later in life.

BORN: **EARLY FIRST CENTURY**
DIED: **MID-LATE FIRST CENTURY**
FEAST: **JULY 29**
PATRON OF COOKS, HOUSEKEEPERS, STAY-AT-HOME PARENTS, ANXIETY, SERVERS

THE SHORT STORY—Jesus was friends with the siblings Lazarus, Martha, and Mary, and the Gospels tell of him going to visit them. One visit involves Martha being extremely busy as she takes care of Jesus, serving and managing the house while her sister, Mary, simply sits and listens to Jesus. When she complains about her sister's lack of help, Jesus tells Martha that he knows she is worried about many things and asks her to instead focus on his presence.

BY SHANNON W. SCHMIDT

Even though St. Martha is the patron saint of cooks and servants, she should really be the patron saint of tired parents, social workers, medical workers, social justice advocates, and not-for-profit employees. Basically anyone else who scrolls through social media feeds for self-care tips on a regular basis.

The popular narrative about Martha always contrasts her with her sister, Mary. Martha is the one who missed the boat on Jesus because she was too busy working instead of listening to his teaching. Therefore, prayer and contemplation must be better than good works.

But that narrative is, in this author's not-so-humble opinion, lazy. It ignores the fact that Martha, like Sarah and Abraham, was practicing sacred hospitality to her guest. God is in her midst and she does what a righteous Jewish woman should. Mary, at least from the outside, is the slacker who is disobedient. Women, though allowed to learn from a rabbi, were not generally taken on as disciples. By sitting at Jesus's feet, Mary is claiming a place that, from Martha's perspective, she has no right to claim.

But like all things in God's plan, it is the interior life that holds the key to the story.

Martha, we read in Luke 10:40, was "burdened with much serving" (NABRE). That should sound familiar to anyone who's ever felt the need for a mental health day. And like any burned-out person, she wonders why no one is helping.

But notice that what she asks of Jesus is born from that burden. It is a question about her identity and worth in his eyes. Of why Mary gets treated with love and care and Martha is left alone.

She asks, "Do you not care?" Not "Why are you letting her sit at your feet?" But "Why don't you care about me? Don't you see me working as hard as I can for you? Don't you care that I love you?"

Jesus responds by calling out her anxiety and worry. She has her priorities inverted. In contrast to the humble service of Abraham and Sarah, Martha's work has become a chore that makes her less attentive to God's presence in front of her, rather than more aware of God's goodness. Like any disciple who undertakes service without a foundation in a relationship with Jesus, Martha has burned out.

Even though she is serving the Lord, she thinks that is the same as loving him. Of course, Jesus cares about Martha, but her identity and worth don't come from what she does for Jesus. They come first from her relationship with him.

Fortunately, Martha's story does not end in burnout and anger. When next we meet her, she's still hustling, but this time it's out the door to meet Jesus on the road.

Her brother, Lazarus, has died and when she sees him now, she doesn't make the same mistake. She knows that, even in her grief, going out to find the Lord has to be her first priority. Even though Jesus is two days late (John 11:6 NABRE), even though she asked him to heal Lazarus from his illness, she doesn't scold him or ask questions. She trusts him.

So when this time Jesus asks her a question, she responds with unflinching faith in who he is. "Yes, Lord. I have come to believe that you are the Messiah, the Son of God, the one who is coming into the world" (John 11:27 NABRE). She makes the most profound statement of faith found in John's Gospel. Martha is no longer burdened. She is the one who sees exactly who Jesus is when everyone else cannot.

Of course, we know what comes next. Lazarus is raised. The people are astonished. Leaders feel threatened. This is the crescendo leading into the Passion.

And where do we find Martha?

Once again, she is serving at the table. Her work has not changed from the outside, but her interior journey has changed everything. It was never the work itself that was the problem. Rather her intimacy with Christ, her understanding of who he is, and who she is in relation to him, has transformed the meaning of the work.

And because it has been transformed, her work bears fruit for Jesus. The Greek word used to describe Martha's service is *diakoneo,* which is the word for ministry. As Jesus prepares to enter Jerusalem for the last time, Martha ministers to the Lord before his Passion. Her work bears fruit because it is rooted in love.

We all know that God's grace is a gratuitous gift. It cannot be earned. Yet Martha teaches us that those who serve while steeped in prayer bear the fruit of that grace in their service. Grace becomes effective in others' lives through our work.

Martha is the patron of all of those who need a break because she not only sorted out her priorities but also served well. May all those who serve others be steeped in prayer, rooted in love, and bear fruit in all they do.

PRAYER

God of Rest and Renewal,
help us to discover anew the joy of service
which is rooted in a relationship with your Son.

Transform the hearts burdened by service
and the eyes which cannot see their worth as children of God.
Like St. Martha, may we be changed by our encounter with Jesus
and proclaim our faith in you without hesitation.
Teach us what it means to ground ourselves in prayer and love for you
so that our work may bear fruit for your Kingdom.
Make us instruments of your grace so all the world may see your glory. Amen.

SHANNON W. SCHMIDT is a pastoral minister, cohost of the *Plaid Skirts and Basic Black* podcast, and author of the book *Fat Luther, Slim Pickin's: A Black Catholic Celebration of Faith, Tradition, and Diversity*. She lives near Indianapolis with her husband, Eric, and their four children. Follow her on Instagram @teamquarterblack and Twitter @teamquarterblk.

ST. EDITH STEIN

ARTIST'S STATEMENT—As with each icon I paint of people who were modern enough for us to have photographs of them, I chose to use Edith's picture as only one of my references. I wanted to stay consistent with the rest of the icons I paint, in which I base their look primarily on what I can glean from their stories. For this one, I also used my sister as a reference, since Edith is her confirmation saint, and she definitely shares Edith's curiosity and love of knowledge, learning, and teaching. I wanted her expression to be thoughtful, fearful, and determined all at once. She also bears the Star of David patch on her dress for her Jewish heritage, more symbolic than realistic as she likely was

BORN: **OCTOBER 12, 1891**

DIED: **AUGUST 9, 1942**

FEAST: **AUGUST 9**

PATRON OF EUROPE, LOSS OF PARENTS, WORLD YOUTH DAY, CONVERTS

THE SHORT STORY—Edith Stein was born into a German Jewish family in 1891. Though her father died early, her mother encouraged her children to think critically and question their world, and she was able to send Edith to university. Edith was very talented and hardworking when she was young and was excited to go to school. There she became an atheist. At university Edith chose to study philosophy until the beginning of World War I, during which she served as a nurse. She became a university professor, and after reading a biography of St. Teresa of Avila, she became interested in Catholicism. She was baptized not long after and was able to teach at a Dominican school. While in this post, Edith translated books, wrote, and worked closely with other philosophers, but many people dismissed her, and she was denied various opportunities because of her gender and Jewish heritage. She had just been promoted to a new position when, in 1933, she was forced to resign because the Nazis took power. Edith decided to formally enter the religious order of the Discalced (shoeless) Carmelites and took the name Teresa Benedicta of the Cross. She and her sister were transferred to Holland for safety, but still later they were taken to the camps. She was executed in the gas chambers in Auschwitz and canonized eleven years later.

BY CORYNNE STARESINIC

Before she entered the convent, Edith Stein visited her beloved Jewish family one last time in Breslau, Germany. Two days before she left, her brother-in-law confronted her, stating that it seemed she was drawing yet another sharp line—the first being her conversion to Catholicism years earlier—between herself and the Jewish people, who were actively being persecuted by the Nazis.

He asked why, for Edith, must Christ and Carmel happen now? Why should she decide to leave her family during such a gruesome, troubling time?

Why was this decision worth it?

Edith had started grappling with these questions over a decade earlier, when she first knew she would become Catholic. She realized the anguish her conversion would bring her devout Jewish mother and the tension it could bring to her family. She did not take any of it lightly.

I am a convert to Catholicism from evangelicalism. I am wary of comparing my experiences to those of a German Jewish woman who was murdered in the Holocaust. That said, there are particular aspects of Edith's story that I identify with and aspects I aspire to live out, even in some small way.

I know the distress that a conversion can cause. I know what it feels like to have old friends stop speaking to you because you begin to believe in something they think is wrong. I have witnessed loved ones experience pain and anger as a result of my coming home to the Church.

And I have hated it: the emotional estrangement, the tension that came in the years following my confirmation, the constant fear of accidentally triggering an argument that would end it all.

I know what it is like to be asked "Why are you doing this?"

Was my conversion worth it when it prompted the turmoil that it did? Why would I do something that would cause people I love to feel that I have rejected them in some way? Is it even fair of me to ask these questions as the perpetrator of such pain? On days when tensions are running high, I am not so sure.

When Edith wrote of that confrontation with her brother-in-law, she said he could not understand that she saw it all so differently. Sitting on her train leaving home, she said that she felt no great happiness because all that lay behind her was too terrible for anything like that. But she experienced a deep interior peace from God.[14]

By his grace, I know that peace, too. Because when you give your life to Jesus—when you trust that he is your Savior and dearest friend, when you trust that he loves you and every person you know completely, when you take up your cross and try your best to follow him—you are never really abandoning those whom you love.

For Edith, becoming a Carmelite nun was not an act of escapism, of running from the horrors that Jewish people faced. No, for her, it was running right into that suffering, to bring the sweet love of God to those she loved, as a witness and as an intercessor.

During Hitler's rise to power, she wrote to the Pope imploring him to condemn the evils being done to the Jewish people. She wrote a book about growing up in a Jewish family and the peace she encountered there for the sake of the youth who were being brought up in a culture of racial hatred.[15] Edith was a devoted daughter, sister, and aunt. Her sister wrote of how, after she became a nun, Sister Teresa Benedicta of the Cross was still committed to her family, even from afar.

And perhaps most notably, Sister Teresa Benedicta later asked her superior for permission to offer her own life to the heart of Jesus as a spiritual sacrifice of atonement for true peace, to bring an end to the war. She was ready to give her life for the Jewish people.

And she did. She was later murdered in Auschwitz. She loved her people to the end.

As Edith once wrote, living the faith should not mean severing our relationship with the world.[16] There should never be an abandoning of humanity, of anyone God has entrusted to us, when it comes to following Jesus, because he asks us to give our lives for them. And this doesn't mean practicing tough love toward those who believe differently from us and looking down on them in arrogance. It means living as Edith did: being present—in whatever ways we can be and are called to be—to those placed before us.

St. Teresa Benedicta of the Cross embodied Jesus's heroic love to her death, and it led to her life in eternity, where, I have a feeling, she has been reunited with many of those for whom she gave her life.

Before she died she wrote, "Do you want to be totally united to the Crucified? If you are serious about this, you will be present, by the power of His Cross, at every front, at every place of sorrow, bringing to those who suffer comfort, healing, and salvation."[17]

PRAYER

Sister Teresa Benedicta of the Cross,
You aspired to be like Queen Esther, who interceded on behalf of her people.
You offered your life to Jesus to bring peace to the world,
to bring peace to your people, your country, your family.
Pray that I may embody that same heroic love, never failing to account for the oppressed and the suffering in my prayers and actions.
For all who are marginalized and oppressed today,
For all who are lonely and isolated,
For all who are impoverished,
For every person I know and love,
Sister Teresa Benedicta of the Cross, pray for us.

CORYNNE STARESINIC lives in the Northern Kentucky/Cincinnati area with her husband, Nick, and kids. She founded *The Catholic Woman,* wrote *A Place to Belong: Letters from Catholic Women,* and is currently pursuing her master's in theology at the University of Notre Dame.

ST. JANE FRANCES DE CHANTAL

ARTIST'S STATEMENT—Jane had more things taken away from her than many of us could imagine, and in this icon I wanted to show the pain that surely was apparent in her face. But her humor, intelligence, faith, and patience brought her a little peace, and I wanted that tiny joy to be on her face as well. She holds a heart-shaped necklace that represents the loss of her great loves.

BORN: **JANUARY 28, 1572**

DIED: **DECEMBER 13, 1641**

FEAST: **AUGUST 12**

PATRON OF WIDOWS, PARTNERS, PARENTS SEPARATED FROM CHILDREN, LOSS OF PARENTS, IN-LAW PROBLEMS, FORGIVENESS

THE SHORT STORY—Jane was a young mother who married an aristocrat she was deeply in love with. She personally cleaned up the family finances and dealt with a cruel father-in-law. When her husband died in a hunting accident, Jane was crushed until she met St. Francis de Sales. Together they established a religious order for women who had been turned away from other groups because of their health, age, or other conditions. Jane suffered the loss of children and other family members, lived through the plague, gave away anything she could in the service of others, and lived constantly with a sense of humor and positivity. Because of this and her faith, not only was she able to win over her father-in-law but she was also able to forgive the man who killed her husband.

BY STINA KIELSMEIER-COOK

At first glance St. Jane de Chantal and I couldn't be any more different. She was alive in the sixteenth and seventeenth centuries, a child of privilege in feudal France and a devoted Catholic woman of faith. I am a Protestant Christian living in the American Midwest in the twenty-first century, and I often have a hard time getting to church on Sunday mornings. But it turns out that Jane and I do have a few things in common: we are both mothers, and we struggle with doubt and depression.

Despite her doubts Jane changed the world by cofounding a

monastic order that encourages all people to "be who you are and be that well." After her husband died in a tragic accident, Jane wanted to join a convent, but religious life wasn't open to widows or middle-aged mothers like her. When Jane met Frances de Sales, they decided to create something new: a monastic community that welcomed women who were rejected by other orders. They were inspired by the biblical relationship between Mary and Elizabeth, in which two pregnant women prophesied over each other, and named their order the Congregation of the Visitation of Holy Mary.

A monastic order for the rejects, no wonder I have a soft spot for St. Jane! She is a saint who knew God could use imperfect people, who navigated multiple callings to motherhood and monasticism, and who persevered in faith anyway.

I first learned about Jane from the Visitation Sisters who live down the street from me in my Minneapolis neighborhood. I was immediately attracted to the Salesian spirituality practiced by the Vis Sisters, who exuded gentle humor and hospitality to all who knocked on their front door. From them I learned that Jane was a shrewd businesswoman who managed the finances of her late husband's estate and provided regularly for the poor. Her life was filled with losses, including the early death of several of her children. Still, she got things done in an era of the bubonic plague and vast social inequality, founding seventy monasteries before her death.

Despite all her accomplishments, Jane experienced an arid prayer life at times. She is quoted as saying, "Delight in prayer is no measure of our love of God."[18] Instead she stressed the importance of acting in faithfulness even when we don't feel like it. She battled scrupulosity but taught the importance of "gentleness of heart" toward oneself and one's neighbor. When we are so concerned with our own imperfections, it becomes difficult to turn outward and love the people around us. "In loving God in our neighbor," Jane said, "we can never make a mistake!"[19]

St. Vincent de Paul wrote that Jane "was full of faith, yet all her life had been tormented by thoughts against it."[20] Some biographers wonder if Jane suffered from clinical depression in her later years. The fact that she had intense doubts yet was also full of faith seems paradoxical. Jane was a mother, like me, juggling childcare and back-to-school nights and balancing the checkbook. (Unlike me, she didn't have access to antidepressants.) She embodies something her pal St. Francis de Sales once wrote her in a letter: "I am as human as anyone could possibly be." And still the Catholic Church considers her a saint.

Her imperfection is a comfort to me today. It's from saints like Jane that we learn what holiness looks like. As Robert Ellsberg writes, it's "in the choices they made; in their struggles to be faithful, even in the face of doubts and disappointments; in their everyday victories over pride and selfishness; in their daily efforts to be more truthful, loving, and brave."[21]

PRAYER

Dear God, thank you for saints like Jane who know how difficult prayer can be when our hearts feel cold, unsure, or unknown. St. Jane, is prayer any easier for you now? I hope so. Pray for us, that we might care for our neighbors as we would for Christ, like you did, even when we don't feel like it. Help us laugh at our mistakes, keep moving forward in times of loss, and hold tight to our last mustard seed of faith when despair encircles us. Inspire in us a gentleness of heart toward all our imperfections and teach us to turn ever outward with God's love. Amen.

STINA KIELSMEIER-COOK is a writer from Minneapolis. She is the author of the spiritual memoir *Blessed Are the Nones: Mixed-Faith Marriage and My Search for Spiritual Community.* Connect with her at stinakc.com.

STELLA MARIS

FEAST: **SEPTEMBER 27**

MARIAN DEVOTION

THE SHORT STORY—In the fifth century, St. Jerome translated Mary's Hebrew name, Miryam, into the Latin *stilla maris,* which means "drop in the ocean." This was later misread as *stella maris,* meaning "star of the sea." This devotion caught on, however, as St. Paschasius Radbertus, St. Bernard of Clairvaux, St. Anthony of Padua, St. Louis de Montfort, and Pope Pius XII all wrote on and were inspired by this title. Stella Maris is used to describe Mary as a guide through the storms of our lives, a directing beacon to Jesus, a calmer of storms, and an anchoring star to look to no matter what else has overtaken us. It has long been popular with actual sailors as well, and she has become known as protectoress of the ocean.

BY NYA ABERNATHY

Our Lady Star of the Sea is an accidental wonder. Thanks to a scribal error, *stilla maris,* "drop in the sea," became *stella maris,* "star of the sea." Many loved this "error," finding blessed meaning in the Mother of God presenting herself as the One of Stardust and Water.

Have you ever experienced an "error"? Have you experienced

ARTIST'S STATEMENT—Mary is depicted here with hair like the waves of the sea, and with many tattoos of the ocean life she protects in the style of the tattoos of the sailors also under her protection. She is crowned with beautiful items produced by the sea and has a compass as her halo. She also holds a sea turtle, ensnared in pollution, and looks to the viewer for an answer to such cruelty.

an "accident" where you ended up somewhere or next to someone or doing something you hadn't set out toward, but once you arrived at that moment, it turned out to be just what you needed? Maybe it almost felt like you'd been guided there.

Once, while visiting Quebec, I stopped at the basilica of St. Anne. The material evidence of healings that people experienced at her shrine overwhelmed me. I wondered how many who had sailed on the roughest seas of life came to this basilica—maybe some even accidentally—and found the light of healing. Nearly a decade after my visit, I misremembered the shrine as being for Mary. It wasn't until I researched the basilica's history that I realized my memory had replaced the unknown-to-me St. Anne—notably the grandmother of Jesus—with the recognizable Virgin Mary. An error. A blessed one for me.

Just as people used the stars to navigate the waters, Our Lady serves as a guide through the seas of life. Like children, we experience her gentle, maternal guidance on clear and easy days, and so we also trust her and lean into her arms on heartbreaking, stormy ones.

I know the storms of life. Most of us do. With clouds of doubt and despair, pain and anxiety blanketing the sky, you and I have squinted to see just one light, any light—even a hint—so we can trust the storm is *actively* passing. And even more than that, we look for guidance to navigate our way through and beyond the storm safely.

Through my Afro-Cuban heritage, I learned of the faith tradition Santeria, which pointed me to a figure called Yemaya. Similar to the Blessed Virgin as an expression of the holy maternal feminine, Yemaya is understood by West African cosmology to be the birther of celestial bodies and of the waters, who also protects humans, her children. She and Our Lady Star of the Sea both have stories connecting them to the stars, the waters, and maternal care. These shared elements have served as guides for me as I navigated my faith and experience of God through what seemed like starless nights. Our Lady reminds me that in the middle of the sea, where we are unmoored from what's familiar, maternal care full of counsel and wonder are always present.

Our Lady tells of her love by water and stars, by guidance and care. She knows where you've come from. She knows the waters of the womb you were conceived in and emerged from, bringing you into this life. Our Lady knows that you were born into the midst of a raging sea that is this world, and that you are no accident, dear one. This is the brightest beacon through the clouds of any storm: you are beloved.

Our Lady fiercely loves us and all creation. Often we humans separate our lives from the water and the stars. We sometimes feel like we've ended up here by accident, that we were set adrift with no compass, no care, and no light guiding us through the vastness of creation. But we are *from* the waters and stars, and when we are guided by Our Lady Star of the Sea's maternal care, we can create a sustaining relationship with the whole of creation.

If you're needing some guidance from her, just listen. She's calling to us because *she* wants to be known. *I am mother and protector, wisdom and guide. And I love you.* Look up and see the beams of light from her guiding star, the compass in her crown giving direction, and the care for the sea and the seafarer tattooed on her skin. Rest in her arms as she rocks you like the gentle waves on a clear night. Delight with her as she introduces you to your kin: the waters, the algae, the moss, and the turtle. *I care for each of you and desire harmony and communal flourishing.*

PRAYER

Our Lady Star of the Sea
Full of guidance and care
Secure with anchoring wisdom and presence

Hold us in the waves of your love
When the cloudy storms of life block every light
May your guiding star twinkle through, reminding us of your presence

Let your love wash over us like the waters abundant with our aquatic kin.
May we remember we are not the only ones who are loved,
We are family to the whole of creation

While the journey may be uncharted, we expect accidental wonder and graces because we have found this wonder and this grace in you.

Our mother and protector, wisdom and guide, may we know and be known by your divine love.

NYA ABERNATHY is a public educator and founder of the Dignity Effect, as well as a speaker, writer, and lover of the cosmos. She guides humans in experiential learning with grace, accountability, and hope toward relational well-being that is anchored in dignity. You can find more of Nya's writing on Substack in her publication *Of Earth & Of Stars*.

ST. MONICA

BORN: **~332**

DIED: **387**

FEAST: **AUGUST 27**

PATRON OF MOTHERS, WIVES, ABUSE SURVIVORS, DIFFICULT MARRIAGES

THE SHORT STORY—Monica was married when she was very young to a Roman officer who lived in her hometown. He was annoyed by her Christian habits, prayers, and actions; was likely abusive to her; and cheated on her multiple times. He and his mother were cruel to Monica despite her patience and holiness. She also suffered the losses of children who died at birth—only three survived past childhood; the eldest was the future St. Augustine of Hippo. Augustine, however, lived the opposite of a saintly life in his youth, and Monica wept for him nightly. She worried about his behavior and choices, and her anxiety peaked when he returned from university and she found that his beliefs had taken him even further from her. By then Monica's husband and in-laws had passed away, but miraculously, her patience, endurance, and love had converted them. Her husband was baptized a year before his death. Augustine, however, still worried her endlessly, especially when he tricked her and lied, setting sail for Rome to continue his studies. Monica decided to follow her son to Italy, and it was there that she met St. Ambrose, who

ARTIST'S STATEMENT—Monica's grief, disappointment, and "weepiness" are well known. Her distress over her son's way of living and lack of faith consumed her for many years. However, we must remember that she was also strong enough to endure. She carried herself well despite her mourning and still showed up to her life and for others every day, never giving up. I wanted her to appear like this in her icon, with an arrow-shaped pendant resembling the points that also pierced Mary's heart in sorrow over her son.

became her close friend and adviser. Augustine had come to know him as well and respected him deeply, resulting in his own eventual conversion. Monica and Augustine lived together happily for six months. Augustine was baptized and began to write his *Confessions,* and on her journey back to Africa, Monica died.

BY TSH OXENREIDER

If there was ever a saint for modern mothers of strong-willed children or wives in challenging marriages, it's our friend Monica. Her endurance in running the earthly race, steadfastness in prayer, and patience with those God placed in her life provides a model for any of us in need of daily miracles. This nomadic woman, who lived under the thumb of the Roman Empire, endured more than most of us probably ever will in our comfortable modern era. We would do well both to mimic her posture toward our great God, who can do all things, and to ask for her intercession as we seek to do this work of prayer, again and again, day after day, possibly for years without any signs of fruit.

Think of Monica's daily life: feeding and caring for a husband who showed no love for her, living with a nagging mother-in-law who joined his cause, and nurturing young children who may or may not survive to their next birthday. After her oldest living child showed remarkable acumen and talent, he squandered his gifts on vile, momentary pleasures, ignoring her pleas and scoffing at her piety. For years Augustine wandered the Roman Empire, indulging in stolen food, drink, and sex. When his intelligence matched his freedom, instead of learning from his devoted mother, he joined a cult. He even determined to escape the influence of his mother by sailing as far away as possible within the empire, lying to her about his departure and absconding in the night.

Do we know of any moments of Monica's despair, complaining to God that He doesn't work the way she wants? Do we see her throw in the towel and give up, declaring her son and husband lost causes? Since she was human, undoubtedly there were days—maybe even years—that she felt despondency down to her bones. *Where is God?* she might have asked. *If He is good, why does He ignore my pleas and prayers for salvation? Do my prayers and persistence even matter?*

She might very well have thought these things, because she was a wife and a mother, a human being without the omniscience or omnipotence of God. But her tenacity ultimately prevailed over any despair. Her husband and mother-in-law both converted before their deaths, thanks to her prayerful endurance. And we know what ultimately became of her wayward son—not only his salvation but true conversion. He became a prolific writer and bishop, and even a Doctor of the Church. We as a Church would not be what we are today without St. Augustine's writing, coming from a changed heart, which he claims was the result of his mother's fervent, pleading, never-stopping prayer. An unremarkable peasant woman with a difficult family changed the course of the Church, and therefore history, by leading an indefatigable life of prayer.

What could we learn from her example for our ordinary lives today? How might St. Monica's life encourage us to live well where God has us, no matter our circumstance?

I am a somewhat recent convert, a newer Catholic after forty-plus years of dedicated Protestantism. My family of five entered the Church together, which meant that our children were sixteen, thirteen, and ten when they were informed that we, as a family, would become Catholic. If you are well versed in the habits of adolescents, you know they don't often take kindly, and without reluctance, to changes made on their behalf—especially ones that alter what they've always known and ask them to participate with a hefty measure of faith. Even without a sudden familial shift in worldview, the teen years are ripe with questions: from *Who am I?* to *Who is God?*, from *Is any of this I've been taught even real?* to *What's the point of life if I can't just do what I want?*

I've found St. Monica, my confirmation saint, to be a kind companion for the journey of mothering teenage children. She knows well the daily challenge of letting go, trusting God with our children who make choices we can't control, and pouring love into precious souls who may or may not be thrilled to receive it. She didn't know what would become of her eventually saintly son, yet she persevered in faith, understanding that her job as a mother was obedience, day after day, again and again. She cried out to God for her son's soul, knowing that God was, is, and always will be a good Father. She mothered well through her daily endurance. We, like Monica, must live without a guarantee for our children, but we do have the ability to fall on our knees, daily, in hopeful trust that God is good and loves our children more than we ever could.

PRAYER

St. Monica, teach us to persist in faithful prayer as you did for your son. Help us to model patience, love, and peace so that we may point those God has put in our lives—even our challenging family members—to His son, Jesus. We are grateful for your earthly example. Amen.

TSH OXENREIDER is the author of several nonfiction books, including *At Home in the World, Shadow & Light,* and *Bitter & Sweet.* A longtime podcaster, she currently cohosts the show *A Drink with a Friend* and writes the popular Substack newsletter *The Commonplace.* Her other hats include travel guide, high school English teacher, and mother to two teens and a tween. Tsh is currently writing her first novel from her backyard trailer-turned-office in a small town north of Austin, Texas.

ST. TERESA OF CALCUTTA

ARTIST'S STATEMENT—Above all, I wanted Mother Teresa's expression in this icon to be one of kindness. She is disheartened by the conditions of those who are suffering, but still has courage, hope, and love. Her signature striped habit is found in the pattern of her scarf, with the cross found on her earrings.

BORN: **AUGUST 26, 1910**

DIED: **SEPTEMBER 5, 1997**

FEAST: **SEPTEMBER 5**

PATRON OF THE FORGOTTEN AND UNLOVED, POVERTY, ILLNESS, WORLD YOUTH DAY

THE SHORT STORY—Born in Albania, Teresa went to Ireland to enter religious life and then went to India, where she taught at a school near her convent. She was sent to Calcutta, where she taught at a high school for the poorest families in the area. She soon became the school's principal and sincerely believed that she could alleviate the girls' poverty through their thorough education and the opportunities that would come as a result. Teresa's life changed forever, though, on a train trip to a retreat when she believed God was calling her to a new mission—to aid the sick and dying on the streets. After nearly two years she set out, spending some months in medical training. She was joined by several other women, with whom she founded a community that became known as the Missionaries of Charity. Teresa and the sisters owned nothing and lived in poverty like those they served. Soon she opened her first hospice ministry and began establishing outreach centers for those with leprosy, as well as a home for orphaned or homeless children. Her Missionaries expanded internationally; they cared for people with AIDS, addicts, victims of natural disasters, refugees, and those suffering from illnesses and disabilities. She also traveled to war zones to personally rescue children, assist victims of radiation and natural disasters, and begin aid projects in communist countries, among many other things. Teresa was recognized for her efforts in several ways, including the Nobel Peace Prize in 1979.

BY RAKHI MCCORMICK

They say the saints choose you. That certainly seems the case for how St. Teresa of Calcutta became intertwined within my own life. Because of her work serving the poorest of the poor in the city my parents grew up in, I'd heard of her throughout my life but never much talked about or thought of her beyond the world's admiration of her humanitarian work. Certainly we, as a Hindu family, didn't discuss her Catholic faith or how it was the foundation of all she did.

It wasn't until her death on my birthday in 1997, a little over a year after my own conversion, that my connection with her began to grow stronger. She was suddenly talked about everywhere I was. What struck me most was the way she'd cared for the forgotten and dying on the streets. Mother Teresa took in and treated those who had no one to care for them, the ones left as disposable. It didn't matter to her whether they professed a faith in Christ. To her they were Christ. She is sometimes credited with the idea that it isn't necessary for Hindus to become Christian; that to honor God, they should be the best Hindus they can be. This perspective has come under scrutiny, of course, with some accusing her of promoting universalism and straying from Catholic doctrine.

I think, however, if we examine it closely, we see that St. Teresa's whole life is intimately rooted in the person of Jesus Christ. In that light her statements about Hindu faith and Christianity, if she even actually made them, seem to me to be an understanding that it is God who reveals His Son to us. It is the Spirit that calls people to conversion. It reveals to us the possibility that in allowing others to seek after God in their own tradition, while accompanying them with the light of Christ present in our own lives, we leave room for the Spirit to work without our manufactured encounters. In this sense Mother Teresa was not so much a universalist as she was perhaps intuitive about the work of the Spirit in the lives of those she was serving. This thought is a powerful example for us in this modern age, when more than a few people seem to favor arguing people into the Church and manipulating others into a relationship with Jesus.

The issue of universalism aside, there are two situations from her life that make St. Teresa of Calcutta such a compelling figure in this age. The first is the "call within a call" that led her to create the Missionaries of Charity, without which we may never have known Teresa at all. This idea—that despite her having taken vows with the Sisters of Loretto, God might be calling her to leave and begin something entirely new—gives us much-needed permission to not feel stuck in one place our whole lives. It allows us to prayerfully leave behind a part of our lives for something else we are being called to. This bold move shows us we are not defined or constricted by our work, our allegiances, or our callings. It is possible for us to pivot and respond to the Spirit; in fact, it is essential for us to do so.

As St. Teresa of Calcutta has pursued me over the years, perhaps her greatest lesson has come from the posthumous discovery that she carried intense pain—a spiritual desolation she felt for a large portion of her life. My melancholic nature tends to linger in dark places. I can often find myself feeling alone, unheard, unseen, and unloved. On good days, even in the silence, I can recall experiences of God that pull me out of that hole, but some days . . . some days I get stuck there. In St. Teresa I have a companion who has intimately struggled with that darkness but kept going on the power of faith that what Christ has promised is real. She reminds me, quite simply, that feelings aren't facts. She was confident not in her own power but in God's, not in her own success but in the fruits that would come from following where the Holy Spirit was leading her. Her relationship with Jesus, even amid her great desolation, helped her keep going on muscle memory. In a world where it is easy to feel beaten down in our faith, to feel like we have been abandoned, it is a great gift St. Teresa of Calcutta has given us—to be a saint for those in darkness, that we might remember the light of Christ within, no matter what.

PRAYER

Gracious and loving God,
Lord of the least,
Shake us from our assuredness
And certainties about where You are found.
Give us eyes to see You in the most unlikely places.
Help us trust that You are at work
In the smallest seeds of longing for something greater
In the turning of a heart toward the idea of You at all.
Let us find Your glory in the seediest alleyways
As well as magnificent cathedrals.
May Your presence in us cry out at the
Sight of You in all we encounter.
Give light to our doubt and disbelief.
Amen.

RAKHI MCCORMICK is a first-generation Indian American and convert from Hinduism who found her way into the Church through a series of invitations, and more than a few leaps of faith. Rakhi's passion is speaking light into darkness, however the Holy Spirit leads. She has a heart for the overlooked and the broken. An advocate for God's mercy and justice, Rakhi uses these inspirations to shape her writing, speaking, and artwork.

ST. LUKE

ARTIST'S STATEMENT—To incorporate Luke's main skills and professions I included in this icon a pen, a brush, and a paint cloth as well as a professional shirt for his physician's job. I wanted his expression to be a kind one because of his Gospel's evident concern for the oppressed populations that Jesus came to serve. His eyes are a clear blue to symbolize a deeper sight that allowed him to find such love and compassion.

BORN: **EARLY FIRST CENTURY**

DIED: **~84**

FEAST: **OCTOBER 18**

PATRON OF ARTISTS, WRITERS, PHYSICIANS AND SURGEONS, LIVESTOCK FARMERS

THE SHORT STORY—Tradition holds that Luke was possibly the only New Testament author who was not Jewish; he was likely born a Greek Gentile in Syria. We can guess this based on his Gospel's wording that seems to identify him as non-Jewish, and because of how many times he mentions Jesus helping or praising Gentiles. We do not find some of those stories in the other Gospels. St. Paul mentions Luke as a physician, and it is possible that this was his trade not by choice but because he had been born an enslaved person and trained in medicine to aid the dominant family. Very likely he never knew Jesus, but he spoke to many people who did, and he became a companion of St. Paul on his journeys. Luke's Gospel is also characterized as the most joyful of the four. Because of the words he chooses and the stories he includes, it is also known as the Gospel of the oppressed—women, the sick, the poor, and foreigners are all shown to be more important to Jesus in Luke's Gospel than in the others. The Book of Luke focuses on mercy and salvation, as well as the importance of the Holy Spirit. He also likely wrote the Acts of the Apostles. His highly educated, precise, and forgiving tone is the same in both books. No one can be sure how Luke died, but tradition holds that he was martyred after what was likely a long life, either in Greece or in what is now France. Luke's symbol is an ox or bull because these animals were traditionally used for sacrifice, and Luke greatly stressed Jesus's sacrifice for the world. Luke is also traditionally believed to have painted the first icons.

BY SOLOME HAILE

Any story—etched into pages or spoken through generations—is refracted through a lens: bent as it traverses a body, a life, a world. This is true of St. Luke as he is believed to have written Luke and Acts.[22] And this is true of me, as I reflect on the life and teachings of Luke. Luke is believed to have been a Gentile man and a physician.

As for myself, the complex matrix of who I am consists of my Blackness, womanhood, and immigrant status, as well as my cisgenderness, middle-classness, straightness (and there are so many more dimensions of identity I am leaving unnamed). These aspects of my identity interact among and beyond one another, together forming the lattice that is my positionality.

But we cannot stop there. I am all the aforementioned and I am a liberationist, Black feminist, and burgeoning womanist. These identities give direction to and make more clear not just the body I navigate the world in but also the world I am moving toward and building along with others. We must be curious about not only what people represent but also what they long and labor for.

Of the four Gospel writers, Luke particularly emphasized food and the Holy Spirit. As I sat with that curious juxtaposition, I wondered what happens when food and the Spirit meet. In a sense I was asking what it means for the tangible and corporeal to meet the intangible and ethereal. And where they meet, there is wholeness: where bodies and souls are not pitted against each other. Rather they meet and form a consummate whole, where the fullness of being human—feeling and thinking, doing and being—can inhabit a body, a community, and a land.

In this I felt an invitation from Luke concerning the work of longing and laboring for liberation. The work of love, which liberation must always be, requires us to be profoundly human. When we are subsumed in and in some ways consumed by pervasive and pernicious systems, it is understandable to think all that can free us is something supernatural. Even those who have preceded us in the constant struggle that is seeking freedom are re-formed in our collective memory as demigods, transcending their humanity. Yet Luke introduces us to a Jesus who was deeply human: sleeping, walking, eating, weeping. This emphasis on the corporeal limitations of Jesus was met with the mysterious and intimate accompaniment of the Spirit—and in this intersection there is an invitation. The labor of liberation is both profusely divine and deeply human work. The Spirit accompanies us in ways that meet and honor the sacred limits of our humanity and join us to the collective sojourn spanning time and space.

But what is this invitation to a person who has all their life been at war with their body? To be woman and Black and dark is to coercively be imbued with theologies and ideologies that make the body, my body, an enemy. My body was a limit I had to push past, an obstacle I had to overcome, a mistake I had to correct. I was at war. It was in the midst of this fighting that Luke's invitation found me and called me into dwelling, embracing, and honoring the sacred home that was the body, my body. This is not to say this journey is beautiful in its pristineness. Rather it is in its messiness, honestness, and humanity that I see so much of the Divine joining us with ourselves, with others, and with the earth. This joining is not a first meeting but a reconnection of what Spirit had always intended.

In my humanity and in the accompaniment of the boundless Spirit, I bring my body in its finitude to the life and words of Luke. For many Luke is the book of Grand Reversals. I need more than a reversal. I need revolution: a complete upheaval of what was and an ushering in of what heals, frees, and loves. Womanism has invited me to desire and demand more. I long for more than "the last shall be first, and first shall be last"—I want the entire hierarchy to be toppled and all to be honored. The violence to cease and healing to begin and life to burst forth. The Christ who slept, walked, ate, and wept invites us into this revolution, this resurrection: where bodies are welcomed and the Spirit is near.

PRAYER

God of Luke,

Piece us together. Show us what it means for love to be made flesh and for bodies, flesh, to be loved. Meet us in our yearning and laboring for liberation, making room for our limitations and inviting us to rest. Imbue us with joy abundant and a grounded peace that brings stillness in the uncertainty.

Asé and Amen.

SOLOME HAILE is a Black, Ethiopian, immigrant woman of faith. She is a person who comes from a people of persistence, tenderness, hospitality, and transformative love: because they are, she is. Currently, she is a sociology PhD student at Princeton University. Her research interests include Black womanhood, critical carceral studies and abolition, gender, Black feminisms/Womanism, and social theory.

ST. CATHERINE OF BOLOGNA

ARTIST'S STATEMENT—In this icon, Catherine is humble and quiet in her expression but her eyes hold a passion for her work. I wanted Catherine's whole energy to be centered on a piece she is painting that is out of view. She described creating as a spiritual process and a work of service to others that is also praise to God. I would say the same if I were asked to describe my own process.

BORN: **SEPTEMBER 8, 1413**

DIED: **MARCH 9, 1463**

FEAST: **MARCH 9**

PATRON OF ARTISTS, LIBERAL ARTS POETS, ANIMAL CARETAKERS, BAKERS

THE SHORT STORY—Catherine was born into a wealthy family in Italy. Because they were friends of the ruling family, Catherine grew up as a lady-in-waiting to the Marquis of Ferrara's wife. At age eleven she was invited to live in the palace and she became close friends with the marquis's daughter. The two had a thorough education and enjoyed learning Latin, playing musical instruments, and painting. When Catherine was fourteen, the marquis's daughter became engaged, and not long after, the marquis's wife was executed, so Catherine decided to leave the royal court and enter religious life. The group she joined founded a monastery of "Poor Clares," named after St. Clare of Assisi. They lived very simple lives, had no possessions, and shared everything. They were also silent for most of the day, listening for what they might be called to do. Despite her wealthy background, Catherine volunteered to be baker, laundress, and animal caretaker. She spent much of her free time writing, illustrating, and constructing poetry. She even illustrated her own five-hundred-page prayer book. Later in life, at the request of Church authorities, Catherine left the convent to found a new community in Bologna. She was put in charge as abbess, even though she preferred a humbler role. Eighteen days after Catherine died, it was discovered that her body had not decomposed, and, now venerated in a church named after her in Bologna, it still has not.

BY JUSTINA KOPP

At first glance St. Catherine of Bologna and I do not have very much in common. I am not an Italian Renaissance-era Poor Clare nun. I am not a mystic. I (and I cannot stress this enough) am not an artist. My day-to-day life is far more chaotic and loud than life in a monastery, thanks to my endlessly energetic quadruplets.

I was immediately struck by the humility and gentle humor with which St. Catherine described herself in the introduction of her text, *The Seven Spiritual Weapons*. She wrote, "I am the least puppy barking under the table of the honorable and refined servants and sisters of the immaculate lamb Christ Jesus." What follows is a profound and important work on the reality of spiritual warfare and how to prepare ourselves for it. Her words are so certain and confident.

In laying out the seven spiritual weapons for battling evil, Catherine explained:

> Whoever from deep within her noble and zealous heart wishes to take up the cross through Jesus Christ our savior who died on the field of battle in order to give us life, let her first take up the arms necessary for such battles and especially those which are treated next in order:
>
> first is diligence;
> second, distrust of self;
> third, confidence in God;
> fourth, memory of his passion;
> fifth, memory of one's own death;
> sixth, memory of the glory of God;
> seventh and last, the authority of Holy Scripture as it gives the example of Christ Jesus in the desert.[23]

To be honest, there was a point when I got really stuck on "distrust of self." I read this book during a time when I was specifically working on believing that I am good and learning to trust myself—after a very long period of ignoring myself and believing that my sins meant I was not good. I have long struggled with scrupulosity, so reading this advice in the context of spiritual warfare was particularly challenging. I felt like I had been tricked and betrayed. Am I good? Could I ever be?

I am currently in graduate school to become a marriage and family therapist. While discussing the role of the therapist, my professor explained the importance of empathetic curiosity with clients. The moment we believe ourselves to be experts in something, we stop being curious because we think we know all there is to know on that subject.

To quote poet David Whyte, "It is not enough to know."

My spiritual director actually shared Whyte's poem "It Is Not Enough" with me a few weeks after I had read St. Catherine's words. Throughout this work, Whyte describes how one must go inward to a place of silence and stillness. He writes, "Even one word will do, / one word or the palm of your hand."[24]

If it is not enough to have all the answers, what is enough? The imagery of self-gift with the outstretched hand or the restraint of just one word suggests an opening of both heart and mind.

What then of that distrust of self? I realized that this call was not a call to self-loathing but rather a call to radical trust in God. I certainly do not and will not know enough, and even if I did, that still would not be enough. St. Catherine says that this distrust of self means we believe that we can never do good on our own without Jesus, who said, "Without me you can do nothing" (John 15:5 NABRE). I am not bad; my goodness comes from Christ within me. St. Catherine was incredibly wise and knowledgeable, affording her all the reasons to be self-assured. Yet she knew it was not enough to know. She lived with a peaceful confidence that God had her and would always have her. In not claiming herself an expert—a stance she very well could have taken by writing on spiritual warfare—she opened herself to His vast goodness and safety. She allowed Him to love her.

One area of St. Catherine's life that I find so moving is her mysticism in the midst of her struggle with spiritual darkness. In one mystical experience while she prayed through the night on Christmas Eve, Mary placed the newborn Jesus in her arms. St. Catherine described how sweet He smelled, how precious He was to behold. She kissed His little face, and He kissed her back. The joy from this experience filled her heart with a happiness that lasted for a long time. With great faith, she herself had gone to that place where everything waits; she had opened herself to the goodness of God, and He consoled her.

St. Catherine's radical confidence in God is truly an example for us all. We live in an age when we walk around with literal computers in our pockets. We carry so much information, but this saint shows us that it is not enough to know. Instead, we are called to trust in God's infinite love and the peace and goodness that can come only from Him. Let us then keep our hands outstretched with the hope that God will be there to hold us, too.

PRAYER

St. Catherine of Bologna, I am not always trusting of the goodness of God. Sometimes, I feel like I am not good at all and feel far from God. Thank you for showing me through your art and writings that you too struggled with darkness and temptation. Your life is an example of what it means to rest in God's love as His beloved, to radically trust in His goodness even in the darkness, and to serve God and others with great humility. Pray for me to have the courage to never let God's hand go and to trust in His abundant goodness, no matter where He calls me.

JUSTINA KOPP lives in the Twin Cities, Minnesota, with her husband, Matthew, and their quadruplet six-year-olds: Cora, Raphael, Theodore, and Benedict. She is a 2013 graduate of the University of St. Thomas in Minnesota, where she concentrated on Catholic Studies and Biology. Justina is currently pursuing a master's degree in Marriage and Family Therapy at St. Mary's University of Minnesota.

ST. MARK JI TIANXIANG

BORN: **1834**

DIED: **JULY 7, 1900**

FEAST: **JULY 9**

PATRON OF THE ADDICTED, DOCTORS, PEOPLE SUFFERING FROM THE OPIOID CRISIS

THE SHORT STORY—Mark Ji was born in southeastern China to a Christian family. He became a successful doctor and remembered his Christian duty by providing free services to patients who could not pay. He was well known and loved within his community until a violent stomach illness in his thirties led him to seek pain relief through opium. His reputation suffered when he soon became addicted to the drug. Mark Ji, believing it was all his fault, went to confession regularly and prayed incessantly for an end to what he was told was a grave sin. After a few years his priest told him to stop coming to confession until he was able to do something about his problem. Shunned by his community and likely in a deteriorating relationship with his family, he still clung to his faith. He continued to attend mass even though he was not allowed to take Communion for the last thirty years of his life. In 1900 Chinese nationalists rounded up non-Chinese and Christian people, including Mark Ji and his family. He was given the chance to be set free if he renounced his faith, but he

ARTIST'S STATEMENT—In this image Mark Ji wears his doctor's coat and a stethoscope, and he is well kept, which I found important to portray in an attempt to counter stereotypes about people suffering from addiction. His face is thin, though, as emaciation is a common side effect of opium abuse, and his expression is one of despair. He looks almost confused, wondering why this would be a burden he was chosen to bear, especially when told it was all his choice, no matter how much he hates it. He carries needles, almost unnoticeably, in his coat pocket, and his shirt is printed with poppies, the plant that produces opium. Despite his best efforts, these are things he cannot hide.

would not. As his entire village was put to death, Mark Ji asked only that he be killed last so that no one else would have to die alone.

BY BETH JENKINS ERNEST

See the saint with the shaky hands, the sunken cheeks, the empty eyes. Look upon the drug-den failure, lighting his pipe yet again with other lost and squandered souls. In him, see the millions with needle-tracked arms, empty bottles under the sink, red-eyed, hungover. Read the opioid prescriptions chiseled on the exhausted brows of men and women, young and old, as the ambulance comes . . . one . . . more . . . time. Hear the cries of the baby neglected, born from a uterus soaked in cocaine. Pity the tired grandparents raising the children of the addicted and the dead. Pray for the frightened child posted as lookout on his drug-laced street, the next generation of the drug economy—his name already signed up for an early casket, a statistic hiding a mother's tears.

See the connecting thread as addiction replicates itself through the ages, as the buying and selling of drugs continues its deadly cycle. Look how, in the nineteenth century, British traders sold India-manufactured opium to merchants in China in exchange for silver with which to purchase Chinese tea and other luxuries. Feel the sorrow of China, hating what opium did to their country, forced by the British Empire to accept the trade. Recognize how, on your street and mine, greed-driven international trade perpetuates the human misery of drug addiction.

The witness of St. Mark Ji Tianxiang speaks loudly through time:

- For all who cry to God in the night, begging for release from addiction's shame, St. Mark Ji cries with you.
- For all who worry that God could never love one who sins

so much, who fails so often, who brings pain to so many, St. Mark Ji is an encourager.

- For any who, in good faith, tried a good thing, but it ended up being a nasty, bad, and hateful thing, St. Mark Ji is a touchstone.
- For you who feel undeserving and cut off from the blessings and comfort of God's community, St. Mark Ji has walked—yea, crawled—this lonely path before you.
- For sinners who fight the good fight within their own bodies and in their own spirits, daily pushed back into the ring only to end up on the ropes yet again, St. Mark Ji says, "O friend, I have been there."
- For you who want so desperately to believe that God will give you the desire of your heart, that you only need knock for the door to be opened, and that all things are possible for those who love the Lord,* yet see only defeat after defeat after endless defeat, St. Mark Ji has already anticipated your every pointed question of Scripture, your every complaint of betrayal by God.
- For every mother, father, sibling, spouse who has run out of compassion and in anger cried, "No more!"—St. Mark Ji doesn't blame you.
- To persecuted Christians, St. Mark Ji says, "Let me wait with you, my friend, for I know all about death. I have been there. I will show you how to die."

St. Mark Ji shook his fist at opium. Perhaps he shook his fist at the Church as he sat watching others receive the sacrament his soul craved, week after month after year after decade. Mark Ji remained faithful, thirsting for God as his body inexplicably thirsted for opium.

To suffer and still believe is a grace from God. To suffer for un-

* Taken from Psalm 37:4, Matthew 7:8, and Romans 8:28.

known reasons, to lose everything one has, and still believe—is a miracle of God. To you, dear sufferer, God says, "Look upon my servant St. Mark Ji. As much as he and those around him believed him to be weak, I redeemed him as my own beloved. Rejoice, for it is not the Church that confers holiness, but I. Upon Mark Ji Tianxiang I poured out my acceptance and honored him every day until his painful end, when I welcomed him into my glory."

PRAYER

God of the long haul, heal, protect, and save all who struggle with addictions. Hear and answer their prayers, their sobs, the desires of their hearts. Cut through the webs of lies and denial that keep them from freedom. Wrap strong arms around family, friends, and colleagues who also suffer. And while you are at it, God, change our world. Change the forces that use violence to foster drug production and control the lives of your beloved in fields, villages, and neighborhoods around the world. Infest your Church with love for and knowledge about any and all who feel cut off from You because of their bodies' cravings. May God forgive us who participate unknowingly in supporting the addictions of God's children. Amen.

BETH JENKINS ERNEST is a writer, editor, spiritual director, and retired pastor living near Grand Rapids, Michigan. She writes fiction, short stories, articles on the ministry, and the random poem.

ST. THÉRÈSE OF LISIEUX

BORN: **JANUARY 2, 1873**

DIED: **SEPTEMBER 30, 1897**

FEAST: **OCTOBER 1**

PATRON OF HIV/AIDS, FRANCE, RUSSIA, AUSTRALIA, BREAST CANCER, ORPHANS, MISSIONS, GARDENS

THE SHORT STORY—Though she did well in class, Thérèse was bullied at school because she was very emotional and sensitive. To make matters worse, her oldest sister, Pauline, who had become a "second mother" to her (after her mother passed when she was four), entered a monastery as a cloistered nun. Thérèse was devastated and soon began to suffer panic and anxiety attacks, as well as many physical illnesses. By 1886 she felt that she'd matured enough to enter the convent herself, but the convent refused her: at thirteen, she was too young. Once she was allowed in, she was reunited with her other sisters who had also joined, but she endured more bullying. When Pauline became the mother superior, Thérèse was asked to remain a novice to make sure the other sisters would not be jealous of her family having so much power in the convent. Though it was a sacrifice, Thérèse was developing what later became known as her "Little Way"—patience, small acts of goodness, taking the fault when accused, and not attempting to assume noble, high positions.

ARTIST'S STATEMENT—I hope Thérèse's expression in this icon will come across differently depending on how the viewer is feeling. On some days, she might seem peaceful—content, enlightened. On others, it may look as if she is doing all she can to keep in her frustration, her sadness, her confusion, and her emotional outbursts. Her tattoo is roses—her special symbol—and she wears glasses symbolic of her writing. She also wears a sweater to shield against the cold while fighting her many illnesses.

Although she tried to hide it from the other sisters, she was in incredible pain for over a year with tuberculosis, and she passed away at the age of twenty-four. She was canonized after many people discovered her writings, and later she was declared a Doctor of the Church.

BY JENNY NUTZMAN

Thérèse and I met over twenty years ago while I prepared for confirmation as a naïve, on-fire Catholic teen. Part of that preparation was choosing a saint to learn about. Looking back, I see that St. Thérèse chose me and not the other way around. She came my way through a friend's simple gift: a copy of her autobiography, *The Story of a Soul,* and a small canvas painting of her.

Within the first few pages of her writing, this saint changed my life. She whispered her little way into my heart, confirming an instinct to love above all else and scattering spiritual rose petals of encouragement along the way. This beautiful soul, unremarkable by the world's standards and in Heaven by the age of twenty-four, became a Doctor of the Church because of the legacy she left not only in word but in deed.

Immediately in *The Story of a Soul,* St. Thérèse wonders why God has preferences, giving different degrees of grace to different people. She finds her answer in nature, recognizing that the variety in a field of flowers is its beauty. To be what we are—however grand, small, flawed, or gifted—living fully as ourselves is how we love Him. And to her, it was always about love. If we love our Father, we love each other. Whether we feel like it or not. In big ways and small. Even when it hurts.

Thérèse assumed her place as His "little one" not with a shrinking meekness, as it could have seemed, but with an audacious trust. For her, this translated into prayers for the desires of her heart that could not be fulfilled. She wished to be a missionary, a priest, a martyr, and more, so she became an intercessor for these vocations, no doubt empowering countless others with her bold prayers.

I believe that the "shower of roses" St. Thérèse promised to pour down from Heaven is critical to our movement in the Church today. This is all Thérèse desired for her time in Heaven: to make others love God as she did. If we are to be effective in the roles that God created us to fill, we must be working from Love.

But we most often live according to our experiences, and not all of us have had the best ones. We don't all trust the love of our Father. We haven't all experienced how insanely awesome that love is. We can't all easily dive into His mercy with the childlike abandon we are invited to. But she does. This is the gem of St. Thérèse's faith. Upon reading her story, you will notice her remarkable humility. (It is truly incredible.) You will learn about her elevator to Heaven. (It is mind-blowingly simple.) But what will shine so bright to you is her understanding that simply being ourselves is the deepest way we can love God. She's praying for us to do exactly that.

When I had this realization, it didn't make me shrink with false humility or offer peace while remaining stagnant. It gave me permission to seek, to be alive in our Father, to continuously grow into my purpose and the creation that I am. For me, a part of that realization is helping others understand that we are not meant to be alone in our joys and struggles. My faith blossomed because it had the space, safety, and freedom to do so. Not everyone has those blessings and I think we can do better by one another. Part of who God created me to be is someone who points out the beauty hidden within His field so that the dandelion doesn't get crushed or the rose cut down. My "little way" is creating new paths where needed so we all can blossom as we were created. This is how I love our Father. St. Thérèse's prayers did that for me. I have so much hope for what they can do for you.

I pray you get to know this powerhouse of a saint, that you are inspired by her "little way," seeing far beyond its seeming simplicity to the awesome trust and love that it grew from. And I pray that you learn through these pages about members of your family in God who you had no idea are rooting for you. Sink your roots deep into God's love, bloom where He's planted you, and look around. You are part of something truly breathtaking.

PRAYER

St. Thérèse, my sister,
You absorbed God's love and you poured it out,
In every little way you could.
You still do, over and over,
With abundant joy,
With abundant trust.
Renew my hope in God's love with your prayers,
Petitioning our Father for me, for grace to know Him as you do.
I want to hear His voice, recognize His prompting,
Follow with childlike abandon wherever He leads.
With abundant joy,
With abundant trust,
Absorbing and pouring out love, over and over, in every little way I can.
Please pray for me, sweet sister, St. Thérèse,
Always.

Amen.

JENNY NUTZMAN is a cradle Catholic who moved around as a child, learning early to adapt and love everyone as they are wherever they are. Her family settled in Sugar Land, Texas, and she graduated from the University of Texas at Austin with a BS in Public Relations. Today you can find Jenny again running around Sugar Land with her awesome husband, four kids, and close family and friends. Even when she is trying to simplify, her life is busy, and she places a lot of trust in the help of our family in Heaven.

UR LADY OF ICTORY

FEAST: **OCTOBER 7**

MARIAN DEVOTION

THE SHORT STORY—The devotion to Our Lady of Victory comes from the devotion to Our Lady of the Rosary. When Mary gave the rosary to St. Dominic as a prayer device, he was able to achieve the success he longed for. Later, when a pope was organizing troops to recapture Christian posts from the Ottoman Empire, he instructed his crew to pray the rosary. They succeeded as well, and Pope Pius V declared that Mary had been the force that led them to victory. He established a feast day to commemorate the battle.

BY ALEX GOTAY, JR.

My father is an atheist and my mother an agnostic. My mother was thirteen when she had my older sister and fifteen when she had my twin brother and me. My twin brother was killed in the womb because my biological father (not my father who raised us) abused my mother while she was pregnant with us. I survived. My mother was a practicing Catholic at the time. I remember her telling me that "those people" at church didn't accept people like "us." She eventually told me that the people she went to church with were . . . less than Christian to her. As a result of how they treated her, she left the faith and has never fully returned.

ARTIST'S STATEMENT—This commission began my goal of creating an image of Mary for every type of person and need. This icon's purpose was to show her in a role other than her usual benign, quiet way. She is ready to fight on behalf of her children, her family, or territory. We often forget the strength and fierce protection Mary offers us as our mother.

I spent a lot of time with my grandparents as a child because of how hard life was at home. I wasn't aware then, but each of my grandmothers prayed the rosary. At the time I didn't know what it was; I would use the string of beads as nunchucks on my sister. My grandmothers would walk around the trailer or the projects (depending on which one I was with) saying, "Santa Maria . . ." I'm sure they were praying for me during this time.

In my childhood and teenage years, my family would tell me that I would "chase death" and I would end up like my biological father or brother (both dead). My life was not easy and it led me to dark places. I remember my first real prayer: "God, if you're real, show me." He did. However, I didn't know what to call Him. I did a long study of the Bible and philosophy, which led me to nondenominational Christianity. I loved it. I volunteered, spoke, did youth ministry, and so on. However, studying the Bible led me to question more.

I was doing a study on chapters 11 and 12 of Revelation and began to wonder about the Ark of the Covenant, which appears in the book. In my research I came across some really good commentaries that I didn't know were Catholic. This led me to study Mary through the Scriptures, beginning in Genesis. One day I took the time to pray through the Magnificat. I sat with Mary and all that was revealed to her for all of mankind in the Scriptures. Eventually, it hit me: Catholics were right about her, but I didn't want to become Catholic because I had been told that "those people don't like us."

Around Christmas, my wife and I were attending a Protestant service and the speaker brought up the Magnificat. He said that Mary was used as an object, and we can be used the same way. I did not agree with that. I asked my wife to read the Magnificat, right there, in the service. She did. After a little while, she turned to me and said the speaker was wrong. Mary is more than an object. We left. The next week I enrolled in RCIA (Rite of Christian Initiation of Adults).

I had been doing *lectio divina*—a practice of prayerfully listening to the words of the Bible—for years, even as a Protestant. Now I started praying with Mary this same way. And I noticed something. Every time Mary appeared, she took on the culture and language of the people she appeared to. In every apparition she dresses and speaks a certain way for a reason. I wondered, How would it look if Mary showed up in America today?

I remember coming to a crossroads in my prayer life. How would I picture Mary? Revelation chapters 11 and 12 show that she is protecting us from the dragon. This is a pretty scary sight. I began picturing her like my own mother, sisters, and the tough women I know and have known through the years. Mary would stand in front of her children, that is, the Church, in a fighting stance. She would be wearing the same dress and makeup that all the girls in my neighborhood would have worn, and she would be fighting just like those girls, too. Just like my mother, who fought for her life when she was a child and who eventually fought for mine. This is a mother that is real to me. A mother that I can see, that would intervene for me, a woman of prayer who would fight for her children. This drew me in. Yes, Mary is gentle, but with the fortitude of an infantry Marine that I served with. She is a mother who fights evil. This is my mother, my mommy, someone personal to me. This image has led me to a deeper understanding of perfect love because *love* is an action word. It is a "yes" given at all costs, and it will fight for what it holds true. This is the love of a perfect Mother to her children . . . Our Lady, pray for us.

PRAYER

Mama Mary,

Not only were you perfectly crafted to love and care for our Lord in a unique way, but you also love us each as we are your children, too. Give us the eyes to see Jesus the way you do. Give us the hands to care for Jesus, His body—your children—as you did. Give us the heart that fully showered our Lord with perfect love, to care for His body, the Church, the way you do. You are our Mother and want what's best for us. May we lean into that love as you guide and protect each one of us in this journey of life. Make us saints who know how to fully show our Lord's face to all in need. May your "yes" to our Lord, be our "yes" to Him every day!

—Amen.

ALEX GOTAY, JR., MTh, MPhil, DMin, is a husband of twenty-three years, father of three boys, convert, dynamic national youth speaker, retreat leader, evangelist, Brazilian jiujitsu black belt, and has spent many years in professional youth ministry.

KATERI AKWITHA

BORN: **1656**

DIED: **APRIL 17, 1680**

FEAST: **JULY 14**

PATRON OF THE ENVIRONMENT, ECOLOGY, INDIGENOUS PEOPLE, EXILES

THE SHORT STORY—Kateri Tekakwitha was born in the Mohawk village of Ossernenon. When she was four years old she contracted smallpox, which scarred her skin. As a result, she wore blankets around her face for years to avoid humiliation. Her entire family was killed by this disease. She was raised by her uncle, the chief, who wanted her to marry and constantly brought her young men to consider. However, she refused all proposals. As punishment, she was given hard work, but she toiled quietly, patiently, and without complaint. When she was nineteen, Kateri converted to Catholicism, taking the name Kateri as the Mohawk form of Catherine, after St. Catherine of Siena. Her decision angered her uncle and neighbors, who were wary of her and spread rumors about her. She fled to a Christian community in Canada to avoid this treatment. There she was known to be very devout and continued to work tirelessly. She passed away at a young age from her poor health caused by the lingering effects of smallpox. Kateri is now known as a patron of the environment, and she was the first Indigenous American to be canonized.

ARTIST'S STATEMENT—Kateri is, in this portrait, doing all she can to protect even one piece of the environment. I wanted her arms around the animal to show her both protecting and caring for it. Her tattoos are symbolic of other natural elements and of her identity as an Indigenous woman. She was known to have had smallpox scars on her face, so I made the texture of her skin uneven. Instead of showing her hiding the scars in embarrassment, though, as she was known to do, I wanted to imagine her proud of her strength, resilience, heritage, and appearance.

BY KIRBY HOBERG

St. Kateri represents the truth that Native people are valuable in the Church. That our perspectives are unique and varied. But she is also the only Native saint currently canonized. Her story can feel like the sole example of what it means to be Native and Catholic. I'm a mixed Native person who is white coded. I am descended from the Ponca of Oklahoma. I share very little culturally or environmentally with St. Kateri. Yet she has always represented something between a whisper and a roar that my Native identity was true and rightfully belonged in the Church and my person. St. Kateri is unequivocally in the Presence of God; a truth her canonization makes undeniable as it is an infallible proclamation.

While her canonization does not excuse the harms done to Native people in the name of evangelization—and the tendency to pardon those evils as worthwhile in order to perform baptisms still does great harm in our Church—it does reflect the truth that God has worked within her. She is a crack in the door for Native people wondering if Catholicism can be a place for us. She was not made a saint; she became a saint. No one can be forced to turn their heart to God.

St. Kateri's agency in her own sanctification must be remembered. Her faith is not the result only of the preaching and love of the Catholic community, as readers of her story are so often led to assume. The community gave direction and guidance to a well of goodness and desire for God already present in her.

This community was composed, significantly, of fellow Indigenous people. They were her neighbors and family after she left her tribe and moved two hundred miles away to a mission. The embrace of aunties who may not be from your natal people is still a significant part of Native culture. The unsaid guidance of aunties in the faith echoes through the ages down to us. It is a reminder that we are, or will be, the aunties of today and future ancestors.

A point often forgotten is that St. Kateri was not the first Catholic in her family. Her mother, Kahenta, was baptized Catholic and educated by French missionaries east of Montreal. We do not know to what extent Kahenta was able to practice her Catholic faith or what her experience of faith was in light of the large-scale continental invasion that was occurring. We don't know what impression of faith she left on her daughter, especially in light of the tragedy that ripped them apart. A severe epidemic of smallpox devastated her village, taking both parents and her baby brother, when St. Kateri was only four. Her smallpox scars are physical reminders of the consequences of contact with colonizers.

Those scars have been carried down the generations with more harms added and untold tragedies unfolding. When Native people interact with the Catholic Church, those scars are still present. Like all injured tissue, they may be hard to move through. They're tough and not always visible. St. Kateri's smallpox marks are evidence of difference, an immediate indication of the horrors and pain she endured. They can be a call to become aware of our own marks, both those that are visible and those better hidden from gaze. For in becoming aware of ourselves we can cultivate a greater understanding and awareness of scars in others.

Not for the purpose of merely noticing, but in order to bring ourselves more fully into communion with one another, a communion still in great need of decolonization and healing.

St. Kateri is a bridge builder in many ways. Her people, the Haudenosaunee, developed the three branches of governing bodies with checks and balances that was adopted in the formation of the fledgling United States of America. The Haudenosaunee to this day stretch across the border between the United States and Canada. They, and St. Kateri in particular, demonstrate that it is possible to stretch beyond the concepts of borders, walls, and us versus them. That we don't have to live in conflict with the environment but have a choice to work cooperatively with it and one another. That it is possible to reach a synthesis, and grow stronger, with each change and challenge.

PRAYER

St. Kateri Takakwitha,
Your life is an invitation, your example a comfort.
Help us to take up your mantle of bridge building.
Bring us to embrace your deep love of Jesus,
while never forgetting to bring our full selves to devotion.
In Jesus's Name,
Amen.

KIRBY HOBERG is a member of the Ponca Tribe of Oklahoma. She is a theater artist living in the Twin Cities of Minnesota raising four young kids. On Instagram @underthyroof.

ST. OLYMPIAS

BORN: **362**

DIED: **JULY 25, 408**

FEAST: **JULY 25**

PATRON OF WIDOWS, ORGANIZERS, ADMINISTRATORS, FRIENDSHIPS, DEACONS, WOMEN IN THE CHURCH

THE SHORT STORY—Olympias was born in what is now Turkey to a wealthy and noble family. Her parents passed away when she was young, however, leaving her an enormous fortune. At age twenty-one she married a prefect named Nebridius, but after only two years Nebridius died. Because of Olympias's wealth, she received many offers of marriage, including one match recommended by the emperor himself. But she refused to remarry. As punishment the emperor took her fortune away from her. Rather than be cowed, Olympias responded to the emperor's threat by telling him to give the money to the Church. Impressed by the principled young noblewoman, Emperor Theodosius gave Olympias's property back to her. She immediately began to distribute her funds to anyone in her community who was in need. Despite her young age, Olympias was consecrated a deaconess. She turned one of her mansions in Constantinople into a monastery, where she and several other female relatives lived—dedicating their lives to monastic prayer, fasting, and caring for the poor. She built a hospital and an orphanage in the city, and she became fast friends with John Chrysostom when he was appointed patriarch of Constantinople. Things took a turn when John Chrysostom

ARTIST'S STATEMENT—Olympias is pictured here with the letters she wrote, saved, and cataloged, as well as a censer—a symbol of the vocation of deacon. She is determined and steadfast in her expression as she was in all of her decisions, and she dares to speak rather than keep her mouth closed.

was exiled from the city in 402 for criticizing Empress Eudoxia. Olympias defended her friend staunchly. In response, the emperor punished Olympias with a fine and disbanded her religious community. Olympias herself was banished twice for her actions, resulting in the loss of her home and the rest of her wealth. Throughout his own exile, John wrote Olympias many tender pastoral letters, encouraging and supporting her just as she had supported him. John passed away while still in exile a year before Olympias's own death.

BY RENÉE DARLINE RODEN

The stories of saints are often stories of great friendships: Francis and Clare, Benedict and Scholastica, or Ignatius and Francis Xavier. Olympias and John Chrysostom may not have had the most famous friendship, but the courageous young deaconess and famous preacher's companionship demonstrates the beauty and power of two souls supporting each other on their path to holiness.

I first found Olympias through John Chrysostom's letters to her, written during his exile. A balm for the soul, they are tender and compassionate and show delicate care for her sorrow and mental anguish. "Despondency for souls is a grievous torture chamber," John wrote. "I will scatter the dust of your despondency, for I know that this dust has resulted from a grievously swelling wound in your soul."[25]

I can relate to some of the anxieties and depressions Olympias felt. Those of us wrestling with worry, a hidden wound, or a hurt that festers in our hearts can imagine the gift it would be to receive such consoling words from a dear friend who knows our struggles. Although these letters are ancient, they show a sensitivity toward Olympias's mental and spiritual health that speaks to those of us wrestling with loneliness and depression today.

Olympias inspires me with her commitment to the Church. She was ordained a deaconess in her early thirties, much earlier than most women were allowed to become deaconesses. Usually women of childbearing age of Olympias's social class would have remarried. But Olympias knew, like the disciple Mary of Bethany, that "one thing was needful."*

In 398, when John Chrysostom became Archbishop of Constantinople, Olympias gained a new neighbor. Her monastery was directly next door to the cathedral and the archbishop's living quarters. They quickly became friends, and Olympias adopted him as her spiritual father. John Chrysostom often ate with Olympias and the other members of her community rather than attending elaborate dinners with wealthy clerics and influential noblemen.

Their friendship reminds me of some of my best friends—the most inspiring people I know—who encourage me in the foolhardy path of pursuing the Gospel and living by the evangelical counsels of poverty, chastity, and obedience. Perhaps building authentic friendships with people tirelessly and passionately pursuing God, who offer hospitality to "the least of these,"† and give up glory and status to pursue holiness, is an underrated yet excellent way to become a saint.

Although I'm from a comfortable, quiet suburb in Minneapolis, I have lived most of my adult life in cities—in New York City and now Chicago—and I have constantly been challenged by passing Christ on the streets: Christ asking for a dollar or a sandwich, Christ overdosing on the sidewalk, Christ pleading for help. John Chrysostom's sermons encouraging his congregation to ignore the poor at the risk of their own damnation speak to me as though they were written seven hours ago, not seventeen hundred years ago. Seeing the pure love that drove John Chrysostom and Olympias to care for the unfortunate around them because the poor are an image of God—not because they are worthy or good or hardworking—has inspired me to accept personal responsibility for my neighbor.

The young American journalist Dorothy Day was inspired by

* Taken from Luke 10:42 KJV.

† Taken from Matt. 25:40 KJV.

the words of John Chrysostom to help found the Catholic Worker movement in 1933. It called upon bishops to emulate John Chrysostom and Olympias and open houses of hospitality for the down-and-out. When the bishops didn't do it, Dorothy did. And many men and women have followed her example. Today there are over 170 houses of hospitality across the United States. Last year I joined the St. Francis Catholic Worker House in Chicago's Uptown neighborhood, a house of hospitality that challenges me each day to live as though the guest on my front porch is Christ.

So often, we try to compromise the Gospel. To bend the demands of charity so that we do not lose our comfort. In John Chrysostom's and Olympias's lives and writings, I found friends who "live the truth as though it were true." Olympias's own life is a testament to her commitment to loving her neighbors, radically, as though we truly do believe they are fellow members in the Body of Christ.

PRAYER

St. Olympias, deaconess and friend, your love for God radiated through your friendship with John Chrysostom. In your joint ministry and life together, you inspired and encouraged each other to live in holiness. Help us to lift up our friends, love them, and cherish them as blessings from God who reveal the face of God for us. You gathered your friends together in hospitality to care for the poor and sick in our communities. May all our relationships inspire us to love the least of our brethren more and more, and may our friendships expand to include the lonely, marginalized, and isolated. St. Olympias, who endured the long loneliness and found the answer in love and a community built on love, pray for us!

RENÉE DARLINE RODEN is a journalist and playwright from Minnesota. She met John Chrysostom and Olympias during her master of Theological Studies degree at the University of Notre Dame. She currently lives at St. Francis Catholic Worker House in Chicago.

THE MYRRHBEARERS

BORN: **FIRST CENTURY**
DIED: **FIRST CENTURY**
FEAST: **SECOND SUNDAY AFTER EASTER**
PATRONS OF MOURNING, HOPE, BURIAL, LOYALTY

THE SHORT STORY—The Myrrhbearers is a name given to the women who came to Jesus's tomb to minister to his body (with myrrh and other spices) for three days after his burial, in accordance with Jewish tradition. Because of this, when they arrived early on the third day, they were the first to be told of Jesus's Resurrection. The accounts in the Gospels differ on which women were present and when, suggesting that they may not all have been there at the same time, or that the roles they played in Jesus's burial differed but were equally important. Regardless, historians agree that because women could not testify in court, and because men would not have invented such an important role for women, the fact that it is recorded makes it certainly true: the women really were the first to see the empty tomb and to meet the risen Lord. Some accounts describe Peter and John running to the tomb, but the women are still described as the first to learn about Jesus's Resurrection. The women present were all important figures throughout Jesus's life; they traveled with the Apostles and provided for all of them during Jesus's

ARTIST'S STATEMENT—In this icon, I hoped to capture as many ideas about the Myrrhbearers as I could in one image, with only three women pictured. I tried to give them differing ages, expressions, and immediate reactions in their first moment realizing what happened to Jesus. It was an enormous revelation for them and extremely difficult to comprehend, but, as theologians have pointed out throughout the Gospels, the women were often the only ones to understand Jesus.

ministry. The women listed in the different Gospel accounts are Mary Magdalene, Jesus's Mother Mary, Mary the wife of Cleopas, Martha and Mary of Bethany, Joanna, Susanna, and Salome, the mother of the Apostles James and John.

BY LAURA KELLY FANUCCI

"Myrrhbearers" is a mysterious mouthful of a term, one I didn't discover until deep in the darkness of the Covid pandemic.

This sacred name is given to the followers of Jesus who cared for his body at his burial, anointing it with sacred oil mixed with bitter myrrh. They were the same women who discovered the empty tomb after his Resurrection. Drawing together different Scripture accounts, the Myrrhbearers include women who are identified (including Mary Magdalene, Mary the mother of Jesus, Susanna, and Salome) as well as other unnamed women from Galilee who had followed Jesus to Jerusalem. Joseph of Arimathea and Nicodemus are also counted among their number for their roles in caring for the body of Jesus after his death.

Orthodox Christians honor these disciples as Myrrhbearers for what they carried. The ordinary faithful who stayed with Jesus to the end (and beyond) are remembered with their own feast day in Pascha, the Orthodox Easter season. But the Myrrhbearers are for all of us who have suffered, who seek healing, and who long for hope against the world's despair.

When I first discovered the Myrrhbearers, I was drawn to them like a magnet. How had I missed the power of the truth that in every Gospel the Resurrection is revealed to the women first? How could I forget, even in the turmoil of recent years, that God can be found in the least likely places?

As soon as I read the word Myrrhbearer, my whole body felt electric. I realized I needed their balm and anointing in my own life. Our world is hungry for healing too, for the sacred touch lost first to social distancing and then to our deepening social divisions. The

Myrrhbearers bring light into darkness, not only to the ragtag band of believers in the earliest community of Christians but also to those of us who still seek life in the shadow of death, scrounging for hope in overlooked corners.

The Myrrhbearers knew grief intimately. They were unafraid to get close to suffering and death, tending to Jesus's bloodied, beaten body after his Crucifixion. They kept showing up when others abandoned, betrayed, or denied him in his darkest hours.

Light bearers. Holy anointers. Faithful followers.

Their quiet adherence to ancient rituals turned into a radical act of discipleship. The Myrrhbearers were called to preach, in word and action, by showing up in the hardest moments and going to the edge of life's limits—exactly where they discovered the stunning reversal brought by the Resurrection.

To follow in their footsteps means to strike out in faith while the world is still dark, the future uncertain, and the way unmarked. To serve when others scatter. To let ourselves be surprised by God and to be sent forth on a new mission of startling hope.

Now I keep the Myrrhbearers close, especially on days when my flame of faith flickers or the world's woes press with unbearable weight. Their steady gazes meet my eyes, urging me to trust despite all evidence to the contrary. Their mouths open to teach me how to speak good news in hard times. Their strong hands show me how to bear whatever bitterness life has given and let it be transformed by God.

The Myrrhbearers ask us to carry our questions as holy offerings, the sacred vessels of faith. No strangers to suffering, they look us full in the face, embracing the brokenness of our own lives.

They go together to the tomb, drawing courage from one another's strength, honoring ancient practices of reverence for bodies, care for the broken, and compassion for those cast aside by society. They teach us what to carry and what to let go.

What have you known of suffering? What healing are you seeking?

Let the Myrrhbearers become companions on your way. They

will bring you the balm of their comfort and the light of their witness. They will not leave you lost, even while it is still dark.

PRAYER

God of mystery and myrrh,
open our eyes
to the wisdom of the Myrrhbearers,
our ancestors in faith.
As we follow in their footsteps,
doing the daily work of discipleship,
seeking to serve you,
offering all that we have
and all that we are,
enliven our faith and enlighten our hearts.
Let the prophetic lives
and courageous love
of the women and men
unafraid to seek and serve you
carry us through our own suffering
while the world is still dark.
We ask this in Jesus's name. Amen.

LAURA KELLY FANUCCI is an author, speaker, and retreat leader. Her books include *Everyday Sacrament: The Messy Grace of Parenting* and *To Bless Our Callings: Prayers, Poems, and Hymns to Celebrate Vocation.* Laura is the founder of MotheringSpirit.com, a collaborative, ecumenical project featuring storytelling from diverse voices on parenting and spirituality shaped by the liturgical seasons.

ST. JUNIA

BORN: **~5**

DIED: **MID-LATE FIRST CENTURY**

FEAST: **MAY 17**

PATRON OF WOMEN LEADERS, WOMEN IN THE CHURCH, WOMEN IN PRISON

THE SHORT STORY—Junia is mentioned only once in the New Testament, in St. Paul's Letter to the Romans, but we can know a good deal about her from just this one account.* First, we know that Junia and a man named Andronicus have been in prison with Paul for their outspoken Christianity, and therefore we know that Junia was considered enough of a threat to the Roman Empire to be imprisoned. Second, she and Andronicus are related to Paul. We aren't sure how, and we aren't sure if Andronicus and Junia were married, siblings, cousins, or some other relation. Next, we know that they have been doing great work. Paul commends them as "outstanding among the apostles." The meaning of Paul's use of the word *apostle* for Junia has been debated because that term has traditionally recognized only the men who held the positions of Jesus's direct Apostles. At one point in history, scribes even tried to add an *s* to her name to make it seem as if Paul was referring to a man—thus suggesting that they were indeed afraid this one sentence could change our traditional understanding. It is still debated today,

* "Greet Andronicus and Junia, my fellow Jews who have been in prison with me. They are outstanding among the apostles, and they were in Christ before I was" (Romans 16:7 NIV).

ARTIST'S STATEMENT—The last thing I wanted was for Junia to appear as a quiet, submissive woman in the background like so many traditional works and icons do. She clearly has some thoughts she is about to make you aware of, her arms are crossed in defiance, and she has, perhaps most powerfully of all, a fearless, confident joy.

but regardless, Junia made an enormous, lasting impact on the foundation of the Church, and likely lost her life for it as a martyr, along with Andronicus.

BY JENNY BOOTH POTTER

This past Sunday my family met up with our good friends at the local pool. It was a perfect Midwest summer day, clear with a slight breeze and a warm sun. In between kids splashing and quite literally melting down, I waited for a moment, for a lull in the conversation, to ask about the name of my friend's youngest daughter, Junia, or June, as they often call her.

"How did you come up with the name Junia? And why?" I asked. Nadia is an Episcopal priest by way of growing up Catholic. Her partner, Steve, is the editor of an ecumenical magazine. Nadia went first. "We always loved the idea of our children having biblical names, so when we found this name and heard the way Paul addressed her, we were sold." "Plus we love June Carter Cash, so that didn't hurt either," added Steve with a grin.

The moment passed and I figured we had moved on when a child cried for a towel and wrapped themselves up a few feet away. Then Steve added one more thought: "Paul didn't defend Junia as an Apostle. He could have. But he just commends her and moves on."

It struck me then, and I still can't get that thought out of my head. It is a powerful choice when one chooses not to start off on the defensive. Perhaps Paul even should have, as many scholars have debated if Paul said what he seems to have said, if he esteemed who he esteemed. But if Junia was who we know her to be—such a threat to the Roman Empire they needed to imprison her, such an asset to the Church that Paul had heard of the work she was doing—choosing to overly hype her up would be kinda odd, don't you think?

For many years I worked at a church that loudly proclaimed it was egalitarian. That it believed women and men were equally able to lead and should lead according to their gifts within the church. It was on the church's website, part of the agreement in the staff handbook, a value critical to becoming a member. It was sometimes argued and defended in sermons or at staff meetings. As a woman who grew up in a church where women were allowed to serve only in children's ministry or women's ministry, I was eager to be at a place so quick to talk of the importance of women leading in every area of the church. They talked and talked and talked about it. However, it was rarely normalized. When a woman preached or led, it stuck out. And it wasn't until many years into my time there that I realized there weren't actually that many women in leadership positions. Or regularly preaching. That the opportunities for women on staff weren't growing; in fact in some ways they were actually declining. Being *about it* had in some way taken the place of just *being it*. Of living it out. Of walking the walk.

St. Junia was clearly a living embodiment of a follower of Jesus. She was not asking for permission to lead, she was following the radical example of Jesus, who welcomed the outcast, the overlooked, the unlikely, the unapproved. And St. Junia seems to me the type of woman who wasn't just trying to be *about* something; she simply embodied her call for leading in the Church by just doing exactly that. Leading.

Thank God for St. Junia's example and witness. As activist and author Marian Wright Edelman brilliantly stated, "It's hard to be what you can't see." I am so grateful for what this one sentence in Paul's letter is for those of us who see ourselves in Junia. Who see the ways our presence or existence does not fit within a certain tradition or hierarchy, but who know we deserve a seat at the table (or are even able to go build a new and bigger table), and live and act according to that inherent dignity and worthiness.

PRAYER

Mother God,

Thank you for the life and legacy of St. Junia. Thank you for the incredible power of her example and the ways her life and existence threatened regimes and systems set up to exclude and dehumanize. Thank you for the message of the Gospel, which is that Jesus's words are truly good news for all people. Like St. Junia, may we embrace that sense of entitlement when we encounter churches and other institutions who feel threatened by our existence, or who preach a gospel that is only good news for some. May we embody this belief in a fresh way. Amen.

JENNY BOOTH POTTER is a creative producer, storyteller, and cohost of *The Next Question,* a web series about expanding our imagination for racial justice. She has co-led racial justice trainings across the country for churches and organizations, and is a founding partner of HerSelf Media, a company that aims to create stories that empower and bring joy to Black women. Jenny's first book is *Doing Nothing Is No Longer an Option: One Woman's Journey into Everyday Antiracism.* You can find her at jennyboothpotter.com. Jenny and her husband make their home outside of Chicago with their two boys and one wild puppy.

ST. MARTIN OF TOURS

ARTIST'S STATEMENT—Riding a motorcycle rather than a horse, which would stand out quite a bit on today's streets, Martin still offers half of his cloak to a man outside of the image. Though it's a puffer coat rather than a cape, Martin also has an image of a goose on his sweatshirt in reference to his hiding place and patronage.

BORN: **316**

DIED: **NOVEMBER 8, 397**

FEAST: **NOVEMBER 11**

PATRON OF POVERTY, FRANCE, GEESE, HORSES, INNKEEPERS, TAILORS, VINEYARDS

THE SHORT STORY—Because Martin's father was a retired soldier, he knew he was going to be forced to enter the army. From the age of ten, though, he told his parents that he wanted to be a Christian. Though Christianity had been legalized only a few years earlier, it still was not widely accepted and his parents begged him to reconsider. Martin was conscripted into the army when he was fifteen. It was while there that he encountered a starved, freezing man begging on the street, and Martin cut his own cloak to clothe the man. Martin dreamed that night of it having been Jesus himself he had clothed, and in the morning he found the full cloak restored. While he was still in the army, it was said that he lived "more like a monk than a soldier." At the end of his career Martin stated that he would no longer fight, or listen to any person other than Jesus. He refused a war bonus and refused to fight in the next battle. Martin's next move was to become a student of Bishop Hilary of Poitiers. He walked the countryside and preached, living for a time on an island. When the city of Tours needed a bishop, Martin refused. The people wanted him in the position, however, so they called him to minister to a sick person. When he found it was a trick, he tried to hide in a barn full of geese! He was made the bishop anyway. Martin filled the role well despite his initial refusal, establishing a parish system to manage his diocese, visiting each parish frequently, and establishing a new monastery in Marmoutier. He made it his mission also to free prisoners, and to stand in the way of a heretical bishop's execution. Because of his opposition,

Martin himself was accused of the same heresy and lost favor with many leaders. He continued to oppose government involvement in Church affairs until he died at the age of eighty, in 397.

BY JULIE CANLIS

I love Martin because I fear confinement. And Martin lived the first half of his life confined.

I fear anything that might limit my options, curtail my freedom, cramp my style. I love to dream big, with no boundaries, no one telling me what is not possible. Yet this impulse can become a devouring monster—devouring others, my contentment, and my inner life.

Martin shows me a different way. The man who changed the face of Europe didn't get started until he was forty. That reminds me that nothing is wasted and we are never too late.

Raised among soldiers and informally schooled in the most elite of Roman garrisons in Europe (Hungary), Martin was destined to be a soldier. Except that, as a boy, he wandered by a church and was entranced by the life he saw happening within. Martin begged his centurion-father to allow him to take early Church vows at the age of ten. He longed with a boy's idealism for the arrival of his sixteenth birthday—the day when he would be a "man" and could choose the adventure and romance of a hermit's life in the desert.

However, his self-made father was not impressed. In fact, in a swift countermove, just before Martin's sixteenth birthday, his father drafted him into the Roman army for a dose of "good sense"—twenty-five years of it. Instead of his having an adventure in the desert for God, soldiers took him away in chains.

We don't know how Martin handled this personal betrayal, this attempted destruction of his idealism, and the dread of twenty-five years in service ahead of him. What is clear is that he somehow faced and integrated his suffering. And so I wonder: How often do our spiritual ideals undercut the ordinary things that truly shape us, and sanctify us? How often are the limitations we avoid our paths to holiness?

Instead of chafing against the conscription, Martin decided to surrender fully to his military enlistment, making it his desert-hermitage. And it was here that Martin learned the core disciplines of poverty, obedience, and chastity—the vows of a Roman soldier that brought true internal freedom. Martin refused to despair, becoming instead an "inner hermit" in the army, giving away all his military earnings, and in one famous incident, cutting his military cloak in half to share with a beggar. The vision he received that night would forever guide him, for it showed him that he had given his cloak to Christ. *He was not off-course. He was right where he was supposed to be.* And in this unusual context, he would learn to imitate Christ, to the point of embracing pacifism in the army.

Finally, at the age of forty, Martin had fulfilled his military service and plunged straight into his lifelong dream of becoming a hermit on a tiny island: Gallinaria. *Alone for Jesus, at last!* And this is another reason I love Martin: old dreams die hard. Martin wanted to pick up where he had left off twenty-five years earlier.

I so empathize with Martin's fear that he had missed out. That his military conscription had been endured (and he had endured it well), but *now* he should make up for lost time. As a young mother, choosing to stay home with four children instead of following an academic career, I cling to Psalm 16:6 (NIV), "The boundary lines have fallen for me in pleasant places." All of us find ourselves "bounded" by even the best of commitments and have to train ourselves to look for the redemption, *which is always offered,* in the midst of falling behind and perceived failure. The best things that happen to us are never grasped after, but are received.

This too makes me wonder: How many of our spiritual ideals are misdirected and bring us tremendous harm? How much of my dreaming is based in reality, and listening to where God has actually placed me, rather than my desire to be somewhere else, or be someone else? It was in the role that Martin most wanted—hermit—that he failed miserably. He almost died on his island from eating poisonous roots (interesting metaphor here!) and was discovered emaciated and exhausted two years later by friends who hauled him back to health and reality.

It was then that Martin began a decade of communal living, where his true spiritual gifts began to emerge, under the constraints of relationships. Only in this setting could his spiritual discernment, powerful leadership, rhythms of prayer, and healing ministry develop. But truth is stranger than fiction: Martin's reputation spread so quickly that a nearby town (Tours, France) wanted him as their bishop, and so they tricked and kidnapped him! But once again, Martin chose to surrender to the new conscription. Now that he was over fifty years old—and tethered to a large church—the desert came to him.

In undertaking his new role, he rejected his posh bishop's quarters and set immediately to building a ramshackle hut at the base of some nearby cliffs. Within days the people of Tours began flocking to their bishop for spiritual direction and advice, and soon eighty men (who normally would have had to go to the desert to take part in this kind of experiment) had gathered around him, looking to share his existence of prayer and fasting. The cliffs, honeycombed with caves and famed for hiding early Christians, were perfect for this budding hermits-in-community life. Instead of the solitude and silence for which Martin had pined all his life, he was establishing something far better.

Those who visited Martin's caves at Marmoutier were forever changed—and I'd like to warrant a guess that it was Martin's inner freedom that drew them. They were drawn to Martin, and also to the community that was gathering around him—trying to imitate his soldierly example of poverty, chastity, and obedience to Christ. Those who visited returned to their homes bringing this communal experiment with them to new areas around the continent, chanting Psalms and prayers as they went. They didn't know it, but they had become monks. (One might say that Western monasticism was in many ways born in a soldier's tent.) Nearly every city in Europe bears witness to these "disciples" of Martin, who built churches, evangelized border peoples, cared for the sick, exorcised evil spirits, and named streets after their mentor. (I lived in a remote area of Scotland that was named in the fifth century Formartine, "for Martin"—an endearing tribute left by St. Ninian from his missionary travels.)

All this flowed from a man who was continually thwarted in his spiritual dreams—both good ones and false ones—but who chose to make his confines occasions for purification and inner freedom. This is why I love Martin: no military draft, no kidnapping, no introverted dream, no "I haven't done anything yet and I'm forty!," no misguided failure made a lasting imprint upon him. Instead, he willed to receive the greater imprint of Christ.

PRAYER

Lord Jesus,

May we never despair at being too late, too old, of having been on the wrong track, having been misguided and even misdirected. There are no obstacles to your redemptive work in our lives. Even our wounds and confinement bring their own secret gifts. Somehow you guide us even by our wounds; and it is by your wounds that we are healed. So we trust you, wounded healer. May your wounds define us more than the wounds we receive from life and from others. We trust that nothing can stop your purposes for us. In your name we offer ourselves to you again, trusting your redemption of all things. Amen.

JULIE CANLIS holds a PhD from the University of St. Andrews in Scotland and is the author of *Calvin's Ladder* and *A Theology of the Ordinary*. She is the liturgical director for Trinity Church in Wenatchee, Washington, teaches at Whitworth University in the theology master of arts program, and runs the nonprofit Godspeed.

ST. ELIZABETH OF HUNGARY

BORN: **JULY 7, 1207**

DIED: **NOVEMBER 17, 1231**

FEAST: **NOVEMBER 17**

PATRON OF BAKERS, WIDOWS, LOSS OF CHILDREN, BRIDES, CHARITIES

THE SHORT STORY—Elizabeth was the daughter of King Andrew II of Hungary. When she was only four years old, she was betrothed and sent away to be raised in the Thuringian court until her marriage. She and her husband, Ludwig, deeply loved each other, and they eventually had three children. In 1223 Elizabeth learned about St. Francis of Assisi. She was so moved by his teachings that she began to live more simply, and she set aside time each day to give bread to the community. In 1226 floods and a famine devastated the area, and Elizabeth took it upon herself to build a hospital and gave away her clothing and other items from the court to help her people. In 1227, however, when Ludwig died of a fever, Elizabeth was completely devastated. Since her eldest son was only five years old, her brother-in-law assumed regency in his place. Because of this, Elizabeth was either driven from her home or voluntarily left because her brother-in-law was not running the castle in a way she approved of. She finally was able to join a group of Third Order Franciscans and served at their hospital until she passed away at the age of twenty-four.

ARTIST'S STATEMENT—Elizabeth looks tired, worn, and distraught from all of the work and tragedy in her life. She clings to the roses from her miracle (when accused of stealing bread from the castle to give away, she opened her bag and only roses fell out). A hairpiece symbolizes her royal crown, her rabbit necklace symbolizes prosperity and gentleness, and her grapevine earrings represent her abundance and connection to Jesus's words.

BY KRISTIN THOMAS SANCKEN

I want to believe that in their devotion to God and subsequent suffering, saints have burned away any of their doubts and are left with hearts that are filled with Jesus's own love. But I struggle with the theology of suffering, and with the story of St. Elizabeth. I recognize something in her story that I see in too many lives of the women around me.

The way we tell a story invites readers to share our judgments about who is virtuous. In one version of the story, St. Elizabeth was a selfless princess who gave away royal goods to the poor. She was unpopular among the courtiers but beloved among those she served. After her death miracles of healing occurred at her grave. The Catholic Church officially recognizes Elizabeth's cause of death as "fever," which makes sense given that she spent her days caring for the sick in a time of plague.

However, the story of St. Elizabeth's self-sacrifice can be seen in a different light. Historical records show that she refused to eat any food in the castle that had been procured by unjust taxes on the poor, which meant she ate very little. She looked to Conrad of Marburg, a papal inquisitor assigned to her region, as her spiritual mentor. Medieval historians document that Conrad was brutal, beating Elizabeth with a stick if she gave away too much money, or if she chose royal duties over listening to his Sunday sermon. Meanwhile, every day she helped almost nine hundred people by caring for them in the hospital and giving them food—all while raising three young children, managing a royal household, and later being a destitute widow. Historians now say that St. Elizabeth died at the age of twenty-four not of fever but of exhaustion and malnourishment. She worked so hard for others that it killed her.

Is this what Jesus calls us to do? Self-sacrifice to the point of an early death? Certainly suffering until death is what Jesus himself did on the cross, and we are called to imitate Him. But why is this sacrifice so regularly recommended to women and not to men?

Why did St. Elizabeth's first cousin, St. Agnes of Bohemia, and her aunt, St. Hedwig, both also become saints for their extreme self-sacrifice, but none of her male relatives did?

Thinking of St. Elizabeth, I remember the times I have stepped outside societal norms to do something faithful to God, yet in the process wore myself down. During the pandemic I started a support system for newly arrived refugee students to help them understand and access online school. I was already doing many things—including my full-time job as a social worker from home, raising two kids, and managing my own feelings about a global pandemic. All I could say to the reporter who came from a national magazine to interview me was "God called me to this." It sounded ridiculous to say out loud, but I had no other explanation. On a national scale, I was criticized for not also creating programs for African American students and for not making the refugee students more integrated with my own white child's support system. When the article came out, I slept for two days. I was exhausted.

Women are expected to help others now just as they were when St. Elizabeth was alive. Yet no matter how much they give away of themselves or their resources, women receive subtle and overt messages that there is always more to be done. Take two of the wealthiest and most generous women of our generation, Dolly Parton and Oprah Winfrey. Dolly has used her substantial fortune to improve childhood literacy with her free-book program and funded research for the Moderna Covid-19 vaccine. Oprah has donated millions to college scholarship programs and women's empowerment nonprofits. Yet both have met criticism for not being more vocal about and not donating more money to issues pertaining to racism.

Do we have to give until we die? Did not Jesus also take naps? Eat food for himself? Cultivate friendships? Receive the hospitality and generosity of others, rather than always give? Why must women identify only with Christ's suffering and not also with his rest and delight? How can women balance Christ's command to his followers to "deny themselves and take up their cross and follow me" (Matthew 16:24, NIV) with the gentle invitation, "come to me, all you that are weary and are carrying heavy burdens, and I will give you rest" (Matt. 11:28 NIV)?

I don't mean to diminish St. Elizabeth's willingness to suffer with others, which is the very definition of compassion. Her suffering helps us to see God's heart for all people, not just the high and mighty. I only wonder if we would still consider her a saint if she had been able to keep others warm without setting herself on fire. I wish someone had protected her, that she had found "refuge under His wings and His faithfulness as a shield" (Psalm 91:4 NIV), and that through rest and God's rejuvenation she could have continued her work of compassion well into old age. I pray for rest for all exhausted, generous, bighearted women everywhere. You do not have to burn out to be a saint.

PRAYER

Dear God,

Like St. Elizabeth of Hungary, sometimes I give too much. Though I know we are all called to servanthood like Christ, I am depleted and exhausted. Help me to see the aspects of God that involve rest, like the sabbath, and when Jesus slips away from the crowds to pray. Let me rest in you.

Amen.

KRISTIN THOMAS SANCKEN is a writer, social worker, and parent based in Charlottesville, Virginia. She was born and raised in Latin America but spent her teen years in Minnesota. Her work has been featured in *The Guardian, Huffington Post, Living Lutheran,* and *Motherly*. You can find more of her work at sancken.com or follow her on Twitter @kristin_sancken.

ST. CATHERINE OF ALEXANDRIA

TIST'S STATEMENT—I wanted an expression for Catherine that was as wary as it was ermined. Though she was fearless in her debate and profession of faith, she was still y a young woman having to face many older men who were so convinced of what they eady believed that it's amazing they even listened to her. She reminded me so much a few women I knew in high school who would debate older male teachers when they not agree that I used them as references for this icon.

BORN: **287**

DIED: **305**

FEAST: **NOVEMBER 25**

PATRON OF STUDENTS, UNMARRIED WOMEN, ARCHIVISTS, SECRETARIES, LIBRARIANS, PHILOSOPHERS

THE SHORT STORY—When Catherine was a teen, she converted to Christianity. She was the daughter of a noble family and had a very thorough education, but her conversion led her to study and learn even more about theology and philosophy. Outraged at the Emperor Maxentius's persecution and murder of Christians, she decided, while still very young, to confront him herself and to tell him that what he was doing was violent and wrong. Unwilling to be told this by a young girl, Maxentius decided to round up all the best scholars and philosophers he knew to debate her, rather than just putting her to death immediately for her crime of being a Christian. To everyone's surprise, Catherine won the debate against fifty or more elderly male philosophers. Because they were so amazed by what Catherine had to say, many of the philosophers converted, and they were executed immediately. Even more enraged by Catherine, Maxentius had her beaten and thrown in jail. He ordered her to be put to death on a wheel that was covered in spikes. She was tortured by it but not killed, so she was finally beheaded.

BY CHRISTENA CLEVELAND, PHD

Over the course of my career, I've taught at more than half a dozen colleges and seminaries. But my absolute favorite appointment was at St. Catherine University in St. Paul, Minnesota. The largest women's university in the United States, "St. Kate's" was named after Catherine of Alexandria, the fourth-century Egyptian philosopher who was martyred for her faithful resistance to an emperor. I loved many things about teaching at St. Kate's. I enjoyed the hearty collegiality I shared with my psychology department colleagues. I appreciated my feminist department chair's staunch commitment to work-life balance—and, having just taught at an overwhelmingly patriarchal evangelical college, I felt energized by the ways in which progressive women's issues were deeply woven into the curriculum.

But the thing I loved most about teaching at St. Kate's was the students. They were plucky, earnest, winsome, and committed—even though during my tenure as a faculty member, the average family income of a St. Kate's student was less than $45,000 per year. In case you're wondering, that's woefully low relative to other college populations. For example, the average student at my previous college was a white Christian from an upper-middle-class upbringing with a six-figure-plus family income and nary a systemic woe. In contrast, the average student in my introductory psychology class at St. Kate's was a Black or Brown woman who possessed a glimmering skin tone that probably looked a lot like St. Catherine of Alexandria's, was often a first-generation immigrant struggling to learn in English, and was the first in her family to attend college.

Because I was a young Black female professor who also physically resembled St. Catherine of Alexandria, the numerous Black and Brown Somali, Eritrean, Ethiopian, Hmong, and Black American students gravitated toward me—filling up my classes and my undergraduate research assistant roster. I certainly enjoyed the plentiful diversity. For one I was stimulated by the religious variation and how it breathed life into our learning and research on cultural psychology. And yet for the first time in my career I was also intimately exposed to a Black and Brown student population that experienced the world very differently than did my Ivy League–educated, ivory-tower-anointed self. We may have looked the same, but because of the oppressive capitalistic system from which I partially benefited, these women were much more likely to die a death as violent as St. Catherine's than was I. My time at St. Kate's was a crucial catalyst in my progression toward a more intersectional practice of racial justice.

To be certain, as a Black American woman, I am the target of a steady stream of violence. And yet, despite our similar skin tones, I could not ignore the ways in which poverty, LGBTQ identities, English-language-learner status, and non-U.S.-citizenship intersected with race and gender to expose my beloved students to exponentially more violence. The kind of systemic violence that kills socioeconomically oppressed Black women who die while giving birth. The kind of systemic violence that perpetuates "honor killings" among Black and Brown women. The kind of systemic violence that often kills Black trans women before they reach the age of thirty-five. The kind of systemic violence that killed Breonna Taylor.

The reality is that many Black and Brown women live and die (and are even murdered) without anyone even remembering their names. To this reality, St. Catherine of Alexandria can intimately relate, for she too lived as a Black woman and was murdered without any official record of her life and death. Though the history books mercilessly excluded her, oral tradition kept St. Catherine alive in the hearts of the people as they honored her legacy by speaking her name and sharing her story across the world and through the generations. I think of this centuries-long oral tradition as the original #SayHerName campaign. Indeed, it was so effective that St. Catherine of Alexandria became one of the most important saints of the fourteenth and fifteenth centuries, even inspiring revolutionaries like Joan of Arc to stand up for their dignity and humanity.

It is said that, at the time of her beheading, one of St. Catherine's final prayers was that God rescue anyone who invoked her name when they sought help. Intersectional at her core, in her own moment of great need, St. Catherine prayed that others' needs would be met. We honor her legacy when we embody intersectional justice and #SayHerName.

PRAYER

Radiant Darkness who shines through all living beings, especially the forgotten Black women like St. Catherine—we turn to You as we practice intersectional justice. May Your Radiance illuminate our pathways as we seek liberation on behalf of all who remain unseen and unnamed by our white patriarchal society. May Your Radiance embolden us as we seek to wisely and humbly collaborate across power differences. May Your Radiance expose the white supremacy that lurks within our thoughts and behaviors. May Your Radiance heal us as we seek to be community healers. May your Radiance call forth the spirits of St. Catherine and her multitude of unnamed sisters. And may you all lovingly haunt us so that we never forget how the Radiant Darkness shines most brightly through the very ones that society despises and casts away.

CHRISTENA CLEVELAND, PHD, is a social psychologist, public theologian, author, and activist. She is the founder and director of the Center for Justice + Renewal and the author of *God Is a Black Woman*.

ST. DYMPHNA

BORN: **SEVENTH CENTURY**

DIED: **SEVENTH CENTURY**

FEAST: **MAY 15**

PATRON OF DEPRESSION, ANXIETY, RUNAWAYS, INCEST

THE SHORT STORY—Dymphna was born in Ireland sometime in the seventh century to a royal family. Though her father was polytheistic, her mother was a Christian and she secretly raised Dymphna to be a Christian as well. By the time she was fourteen, Dymphna had decided she wanted to live for her faith—but not long after, her mother passed away. Her father had loved his wife dearly and soon began to suffer from a variety of mental ailments. To try to help their king, his advisers suggested he remarry. He agreed, but only on the condition that the woman was as beautiful as his wife had been. As the search went on and on without success, he began to lust after his own daughter, who resembled her mother. Dymphna, horrified by her father's proposal of marriage, fled her home with her priest and several loyal servants. They settled in what is now Belgium, and Dymphna was happy for a time as she used her wealth to care for the impoverished and sick people of the town. Dymphna's generosity, including building a hospice, proved to be her end, however. Her father and his assistants were able to trace some of the coins she was using to locate her. Her father ordered the priest's de-

ARTIST'S STATEMENT—Dymphna, often pictured with a scarf around her head, has on a modern version here. She also wears a red necklace symbolizing her manner of death, and she has a semicolon tattoo, used as a symbol for continuing life rather than ending it—which is important for her mental health patronage. I also included a white lily, as she has been given the title Lily of Eire.

capitation while he tried to talk his daughter into coming home with him and accepting marriage. Dymphna still refused, and in anger, her father cut off her head with his sword. She was only fifteen years old. Townspeople who had grown to love her buried the bodies in a nearby cave until a church was built there. People came from all over seeking healing not from physical problems but for their mental health. The town still welcomes pilgrims into their homes today.

BY D. L. MAYFIELD

I came upon St. Dymphna the way so many women do: I was suffering. My oldest child was experiencing so many difficulties in life and was struggling in ways that frightened me. For one summer they barely left their room. Some nights their body would shake with fear. The world to them seemed so cruel: racism, sexism, the ways people refused to take a pandemic seriously, the active shooter drills at school. It all added up to them, and my child didn't want to go out in the world anymore. As a mother, I stood watch. I was with them, comforting them. I shoved down my own terror and anxiety, wishing with every fiber of my being I could take on my child's suffering as my own. But I was powerless to do so.

I was depressed, on top of my usual anxiety disorder. I mentioned to a friend, someone who loves the saints, how despondent I could get at times. "I will pray to St. Dymphna for you," my friend said. "The patron saint of mental illness." I thanked her, my friend who built little altars to Mary on her bedside table, my friend who cursed like a sailor yet prayed like a nineteenth-century Italian grandmother. My friend who always had one or two or more saint medallions tucked into her bra. I didn't know who Dymphna was, and in the depth of my sorrows I didn't care.

Later, when life was starting to get a tiny bit more bearable, I looked Dymphna up. I was, of course, horrified by her story. It sounds like a lot of other stories when it comes to the saints. Young women, valorized for defending their virginal status. Killed by corrupt and cruel men. I was startled by my visceral response to her story. I hated it, and quickly tried to forget it.

Later, while wandering a Catholic grotto during Christmastime, I found myself looking at a row of medallions. I was still sad: for my child, for myself, for a world that seemed so hell-bent on cruelty. I saw a St. Dymphna medallion, which stated she was the patron saint of mental illness. The coin was silver and textured with her face. I was mentally unwell, and I knew it. I bought it, put it in my purse, and I still find it there from time to time.

When I find it at the bottom of my purse, I think about St. Dymphna, the whisper network of women who pray to her, who say her name to one another when the world seems at its bleakest, who hold the suffering of innocents in their minds at all times. And suddenly I realized: Dympnha was never the one who was mentally unwell. It was her father, and all the men who surrounded him—the armies, the advisers—who were. Violent men who took what they wanted by force. The patriarchy, obsessed with power and control, their minds warped by the belief that only they knew what was right.

Dymphna, like myself, like my child, like so many people around the world—is called unwell by a world that runs on cruelty. She remains the saint women pray to when we are overwhelmed by a disordered world. A world run by men who claim God talks only to them. Men who do not care how scary the world is for young women as long as they can continue to be in control. Dymphna is the patron saint of what it feels like to live in a patriarchal society. One that causes so many of us suffering, anxiety, and depression. She is our co-sufferer and our co-laborer. She is mentally well, but the world around her is not. A patron saint for the anxious and depressed. For anyone paying attention.

PRAYER

St. Dymphna, comfort us when we are surrounded by the cruelties baked into the systems that affect us: misogyny, racism, greed, xenophobia, a love of personal liberty and violence over the common good. Help us learn to comfort one another while never losing our spark of justice; help us learn to love ourselves even as the world crumbles around us. The world is cruel but something deep and Divine whispers to us that another world is possible. Help us see glimpses of it in our world today, and in each other.

D. L. MAYFIELD is a writer, sometimes activist, and all-around lonely and religious soul who lives in Portland, Oregon, with her husband and two children. Her most recent book is *Unruly Saint: Dorothy Day's Radical Vision and Its Challenge for Our Times.*

OUR LADY OF GUADALUPE

FEAST: **DECEMBER 12**

MARIAN DEVOTION

THE SHORT STORY—One morning while Juan Diego was on his way to mass, a radiant woman stopped him along the way and introduced herself as St. Mary in his own language. She informed him that she was not only the mother of Jesus but also the mother of all who lived in his land. She told Juan Diego she was to be called "Guadalupe," and she asked him to build a chapel for her on the hill there. Juan took this request to the bishop, who at first didn't believe him, but eventually did—after a miracle involving the image of St. Mary appearing on Juan Diego's clothing and her bringing him roses in winter. Juan Diego's cloak with Mary's image remained on display in a chapel first while the new church was under construction on Tepeyac Hill. When the church was complete, a procession returned the image to the hill. It was then that the first miracle at the image occurred when a participant was injured by an arrow and would have died but recovered fully in sight of the image. The image is still on display there: a young woman in Native dress, who is likely pregnant and has wings that are similar to depictions of the wings of Aztec mythology. At the beginning of the twentieth

ARTIST'S STATEMENT—This image of Our Lady of Guadalupe has certainly generated some of the most controversy of my pieces, likely because it contains so much symbolism. Mary wears traditional Mexican clothing and a flower crown that resembles the rays of light in the original image. She sheds a tear and holds red rosaries over her heart to symbolize her heart bleeding for the people at the border. In place of Satan as a snake, she crushes the border wall itself beneath her feet. She has a tattoo of a rose like the ones she gave Juan Diego in his miracle, and a Mexican boy takes the place of an angel, his wings the colors of the flag, and his expression just as tearful.

century, a bomb went off in the chapel in an attempt to destroy the image, but though everything else was damaged, the image was not. It has since remained perfectly preserved.

BY VICTORIA MASTRANGELO

Our Lady of Guadalupe is my Marian devotion and the image that always comes to my mind when I think of Mary. This is probably because, for me, as a Latina, this image was everywhere—including hanging on the wall in my room by my crucifix. Our Lady's question to St. Juan Diego when he encountered her on his way to help his uncle, "Am I not here, I who am your mother?," is the one I remember when I don't feel close to Mary or when I feel like my prayers are not being heard. I remind myself that of course she's here, precisely as my mother is, in whatever I'm feeling.

But this comfort isn't simply found in Our Lady's words or in the miracles that she provided and continues to provide. Her own encounter with Juan Diego reveals to us the way in which we're called to encounter others. When Mary appeared to Juan, she did so as an Indigenous woman, as someone who looked like him. She also spoke to him in his native tongue. Mary met Juan Diego where he was and brought her message to him in an understandable and relatable way, an approach she has taken throughout history in her various apparitions.

In a world in which we often find ourselves in the echo chambers of social media algorithms that consistently show us things exactly as we view them, it can be easy to feel like preaching the Gospel means using only specific words, images, and references. It can seem like evangelization is best or "right" when it looks like this person's Instagram feed or like that influencer's podcast. It can become a blanket "all good Catholics believe" or "all devout or practicing Christians do" without consideration for the person on the other side of our preaching.

Our world today needs the example of Our Lady of Guadalupe.

We need to ask ourselves if we're trying to reach people as individuals, on their level and in their own "language." Are we using terminology that is unfamiliar or wording that is too formulaic, off-putting, or intimidating? Or are we talking to them from the place of their experience and their understanding? Is our approach coming from a place of familial love prompted by the call to love our neighbor?

When the bishop first ignored Juan's request from Mary and refused to believe him, Juan wanted to give up. He told her to find someone else. He was not capable or worthy enough to complete this mission. However, Mary did not agree, and she not only gave him the same message to deliver but promised a sign to accompany it. How many times do we think that someone is unworthy of being a Christian? How many times do we believe that our own definition of what it means to be "practicing" the faith is the only one and that those outside that definition are unworthy or incapable of being called a Christian?

One of the things that I love about being a teacher is getting to see the unexpected from a student who has been having a hard time understanding something. It's what many call that "lightbulb" moment—when a student who has been struggling with something finally gets it. As a theology teacher, I like best the moments when students who have seen God as distant or have had difficulty in their relationship with Him have a breakthrough experience and are able to see or feel Him, even if just for a moment. It gives them hope.

Helping them navigate that relationship is the great privilege of my job, but it's one that I can do only when I follow Our Lady of Guadalupe's lead. If I just see a kid struggling with her faith and doing all the wrong things, it can be easy to cast her off as uninterested, and to shift my focus to those students already excited about their faith. But telling students that they're wrong or missing something is not going to give them the glimpse of God's love that we're called to be. Providing strict textbook catechism responses to their questions does not meet them where they are or speak in their tongue. Nor does it allow the wiggle room that they need to figure out faith for themselves. What they need is someone who listens, who gently guides, and who has a confidence in them that they don't have in themselves or in their ability to find God. While I may not be their mother, I can still respond to their doubts like Our Lady of Guadalupe, "Am I not here, I, a person who loves you?" Let's all respond in such a way to whomever God puts in our path.

PRAYER

Virgen y Madre,

You appear to your children in ways that we can recognize and understand.

As our perfect mother, you wrap us in your mantle, calm our fears, care for our needs, and give us the confidence to fulfill the mission that God has for us.

Guide us in our own work of ministering to others. Help us to live out this example in our encounters with our neighbors and strangers and enemies and friends.

Help us to love as you do.

Our Lady of Guadalupe, pray for us.

VICTORIA MASTRANGELO is a wife, mother, and high school campus minister and theology teacher in Houston. She also serves as the Church section editor for *FemCatholic* and a freelance writer for other Catholic publications. In her spare time, she loves to read multiple books at once, take her kids to the zoo, and drink way too much coffee. Her favorite saints are Edith Stein, Ignatius of Loyola, Dorothy Day, and John Paul II, which tells you a lot about her spirituality and love of the feminine genius and social justice. You can follow her writing at vmastrangelo.journoportfolio.com or find her on Instagram.

THE VISITATION

ARTIST'S STATEMENT—The goal for this image was to include both babies in the painting as well, and this is done through the women's sonograms. This icon is another one in which I did not want the subjects' expressions to be very clear. Most depictions show the women as overjoyed—which they were—to have both been recipients of miracles. But both also knew that hardships would come their way because of the miracles, and neither knew quite yet the whole of what was to happen.

FEAST: **MAY 31**

MARIAN DEVOTION

THE SHORT STORY—Only the Book of Luke says that John the Baptist was Jesus's relative, the son of Mary's cousin Elizabeth. The story describes a meeting between Mary and Elizabeth while both were pregnant that has come to be known as the Visitation. Elizabeth described feeling John leap in her womb when Mary approached, giving her a sign that John had, even then, recognized Jesus as the Son of God.

BY KELLY SANKOWSKI

It was a cold, dark December evening, and I had just spent an hour waiting in line at the UPS store to ship my family's Christmas presents to them. It was a last-minute delivery because I had been hoping to be able to travel to see them in person and make an exciting announcement. But it was 2020 and we were in the middle of a global pandemic that meant travel was dangerous for ourselves and others, so my husband and I made the excruciating decision to stay home alone for Christmas. I cried, I boxed up the ornaments that announced my first pregnancy, and I stood approximately six feet away from everyone else in that long, cold line, waiting to mail the ornaments instead.

When I got home, my husband and I decided we could not keep this secret any longer. We were hundreds of miles away from family, unsure we totally believed the news ourselves, and we had about a million questions about what to do now. So we set up a FaceTime call with my sister-in-law, Elizabeth, who at the time was pregnant with her third child.

After a few minutes of small talk, we blurted out the news that

I was pregnant, and through the screen we could see Elizabeth bursting into tears of joy as her husband jumped up and down in the background. Meanwhile, according to Elizabeth, her son was dancing in her womb.

We weren't able to physically embrace (in fact, I hadn't hugged anyone other than my husband in a very long time), but at that moment I could understand how Mary and Elizabeth must have felt at the Visitation. As my husband and I began to talk to our loved ones and ask them all of the questions that had been on our minds, we could feel the warmth of their joy enveloping us. Though we were in different phases of life, our shared experience of finding ourselves unexpectedly pregnant in the middle of an already unpredictable and overwhelming time made going through it a little bit more bearable.

Joy has a way of magnifying itself when shared with others—like sunlight reflecting off a mirror and illuminating the whole room. It is only after Mary arrives, bearing Jesus, that John the Baptist leaps in his mother's womb and Elizabeth cries out in joy. It is only after hearing Elizabeth's exclamation that Mary announces, "My soul proclaims the greatness of the Lord" (Luke 1:47 NABRE). That's what I love about Gracie's painting: all four of them are pictured—each a vector of light in his or her own way.

The line in Luke's Gospel just before the story of the Visitation states that "the angel left her" (Luke 1:38 NIV). I imagine in that first moment after the angel Gabriel went away, Mary sat there stunned, perhaps feeling more isolated than ever. But then it dawned on her that she was not alone—the angel told her that Elizabeth too had become miraculously pregnant. So she rushed to see the one person who might be able to understand what she was going through.

Mary was young and betrothed. Elizabeth was beyond normal childbearing age and already in a long-term marriage. But the two women, who for all we know may not have been particularly close before this moment, were now united. If they didn't have each other, no one else would have understood. They each would have been isolated, bearing the brunt of other people's gossip and confusion.

We get only a small snapshot of the relationship between these two women, but I imagine their shared joy carried them through those next three months that they spent together. Perhaps Mary had terrible morning sickness and Elizabeth held her hair as she vomited. As she neared the end of her pregnancy, perhaps Elizabeth had difficulty with everyday tasks as her belly swelled along with her ankles, and Mary did some of her cooking and washing. I imagine that Mary remained there until John was born, holding Elizabeth's hand through the contractions and learning what she could expect in six more months.

What I know for sure is that each other's company—whatever it looked like—made those months infinitely more bearable for each woman. To share each other's joy is perhaps the biggest grace God could have given them as they each sought to follow God's will.

PRAYER

Dear God,

In the times when we feel most alone, please give us the gift of someone with whom we can share our fears and our joys. Help us to be vectors of light in the lives of those around us, knowing that we are all connected through your love. When your plan for us feels daunting, help us to remember that you will always give us the grace we need to follow your will.

Mary, Mother of God, pray for us.

Elizabeth, Mother of John the Baptist, pray for us.

KELLY SANKOWSKI is a freelance writer and editor based in Toledo, Ohio. She currently serves as the body section editor for *FemCatholic* and holds a BA in English and Religious Studies from the University of Virginia, as well as an MA in Theology and Ministry from Boston College. More of her work can be found at kellysankowski.com.

THE HOLY FAMILY

ARTIST'S STATEMENT—Most of all, when making this icon I wanted the Holy Family to appear as natural as possible. They don't all have the same style, expression, or maybe even the same thoughts going through their heads in this moment. That's always how it is with real families. But they are present with one another, and they hold one another

DEVOTION TO MARY, JESUS, AND JOSEPH

FEAST: **SUNDAY AFTER CHRISTMAS**

THE SHORT STORY—Devotion to the Holy Family has existed almost since the very beginning of Christianity, and its popularity has resurfaced every so often with reminders from popes and writers on the importance of family and good family role models. We know that Joseph and Mary trusted each other (Joseph agreeing to stick with Mary), protected each other (fleeing to Egypt), worried about each other (losing Jesus in the temple), and were there for each other in the darkest times (Mary at Jesus's Crucifixion and the death of Joseph).

BY ERICA TIGHE CAMPBELL

When we look to the Holy Family we first see the archetype—in both the Jewish tradition of their time and today—that includes father, mother, and child. They are indeed an example of true love and intimacy, and they model for us the holiness that is born in the ordinary days we spend in our homes. But as we reflect further on the few stories we have of the Holy Family in the Gospels, we unearth something that strikes me as even more profound.

God chose to be born, not only into a family of modest means as opposed to one of power, but also into a situation that was outside Jewish tradition. Mary, still a young woman, was betrothed to Joseph, which meant that they were already married, but not yet living together. It was during this time that she became pregnant. This was just as scandalous then as it would be today—if Joseph was not the father, then who was?

Joseph could have gone to the religious leaders and recounted what had happened. Mary would have then been accused of adultery and likely killed. But we read in Matthew 1:19 that Joseph decided to divorce Mary quietly. This meant that he both was obedient to Jewish law and desired to spare her from public shame. The decision reveals to us that Joseph's compassion was greater than his desire to be seen as a pious man in his community.

But then Joseph was visited by an angel in a dream and told that Mary had conceived a child by the Holy Spirit and that he should care for this child as his own. With his own intimate relationship with God, Joseph was able to trust this message even though he surely did not know what it truly meant. It is through Joseph's trust in God that the Holy Family was formed.

The unconventionality of the Holy Family teaches us that God works through situations that are not ideal. This brings much hope! God is not confined to the way we think things should be. We can trust that God meets us in the surprises and uncertainties of our lives. God chooses the unorthodox and makes it holy.

When I despair that my reality is not as I expected or wanted it to be and attempt to take control rather than trust God's ways, I prohibit Christ from entering my life. It is in trusting the Divine—in all of the mysterious (out of the ordinary) ways—that Christ can enter both my life and the world in the here and now.

Years ago, when I was a young adult living in New York City, I found myself in great despair and darkness. I was living a life that I was ashamed of, and no matter how many times I tried in my own willpower to stop, I could not. I went to confession one day and the priest told me to come back the same time the next week. He became my spiritual director and eventually suggested that alcohol seemed to be the precursor to most of my shame. It took me six months to finally agree with him and seek help. At the time it seemed like the most horrible thing that could happen to me. But in getting sober, I came to understand God in a much more profound way. In order to maintain my sobriety, I had to completely surrender to God's ways. I had no idea what the path forward looked like, but I said yes to the uncertainty and relied on God's mercy.

While Mary was pregnant, she and Joseph went to Bethlehem to be counted in the census. Because of their unfavorable circumstances, Joseph's family did not open their homes to them. It was in this rejection that Jesus was born in the dirty stable where the animals lived.

Christ continues to reveal himself to those who are rejected—either by society or by religion. Christ is comfortable to dwell in the messiness of the world and of our lives. Christ does not hold out for perfect conditions. What good news! Christ does not demand perfection from me. Christ came to me when I was lowly, when I admitted I was powerless, when I opened my hands, and he brought both transformation and healing.

PRAYER

Lord, we pray that your family helps us to see that there is nothing about who we are, or circumstances we could be in that would make you not want to enter our lives. You chose to enter the world in a family that was unconventional. Your parents teach us to act first out of compassion and love for the other and to trust in God, the Father, above all else. I long to have intimacy with you that was modeled in your family and home life. May I see that my way to holiness is in the small, ordinary days of my life and that it is here in my own home that you can mold me into the person you call me to be. Amen.

ERICA TIGHE CAMPBELL is the founder and artist of Be A Heart, a Christian modern lifestyle brand. She is the mother to two young daughters, Frances and Lucille.

ACKNOWLEDGMENTS

Firstly, to the authors of the reflections featured here—you all truly are doing the work of the saints and you give me hope. Your words and reflections are so needed, and the opportunity to work with you on this has been an immense honor.

I need to thank Estee Zandee, my first agent from The Bindery, for coming to me with the idea for this book—it would not exist without you, and I am so grateful for the work you put in to help me figure out where it was going. Thanks also to Andrea Heinecke at The Bindery for your investment in this project and for helping me navigate the whole world of publishing.

To the Convergent team who expressed so much excitement about the idea from the very beginning and brought it into the world—Becky Nesbitt, Leita Williams, Ingrid Beck, Melanie Barreiro, and others—I can't thank you enough for the amazing work you all put in to make this book as impactful as possible.

To the folks at the Columbus College of Art & Design who gave me so many opportunities and resources—I sure strayed from my interior architecture major with this work, but you helped me to be just as successful and prepared anyway.

To all of you who have given me and these ideas a space, whether by asking for interviews and speaking engagements, allowing me to participate in projects, or even just featuring this work in your ministries, schools, or homes, thank you for understanding the power of art. I am honored that you think my work has power, too—keep investing in artists!

To the friends and fans of this project that have been around since day one, you are the reason why these icons and now this book can be possible. Your enthusiasm, support, and love are what enabled me to keep this work going. The way you have spread these images and ideas around is just mind blowing, and it means more to me than I could ever say. There is so much work to be done within the Church, and you all are some of the ones starting that revolution—I admire you so much. I hope that my work has been able to assist in even the smallest way.

Lastly, and most importantly, to my family, who have always been my biggest fans: you encouraged me when I was tasked with school art projects and were willing to go along with me when I wanted to go above and beyond creatively. I certainly wouldn't be here without that. Mom, Dad, and Bing, I love you so much! And to Sam—my darling, my agent, my travel buddy, and life partner—I can't thank you enough. Your support is undying, and I am inspired by you every day.

BIBLIOGRAPHY

Beckwith, John. *Early Christian and Byzantine Art.* New Haven: Yale University Press, 1993.

"Britannica Online." Encyclopædia Britannica. Encyclopædia Britannica, Inc. Accessed February 20, 2023. https://www.britannica.com/topic/Britannica-Online.

Butler, Alban, Paul Burns, Basil Hume, David Hugh Farmer, Eric Hollas, and Peter Doyle. *Butler's Lives of the Saints: New Full Ed.* Collegeville, MN: Burns & Oates, 1997.

"The Catholic Encyclopedia." CATHOLIC ENCYCLOPEDIA: Home, 2021. https://www.newadvent.org/cathen/.

Catholic Online. "Saints & Angels." Catholic Online. Accessed February 20, 2023. https://www.catholic.org/saints/.

"Catholics on the Net." Catholic.net. Accessed February 20, 2023. https://catholic.net/op/sections/53/daily-saints.html.

de Voragine, Jacobus. *The Golden Legend.* Princeton, NJ: Princeton University Press, 1993.

Delaney, John J. *Dictionary of the Saints.* New York: Image, 2005.

Foley, Leonard. *Saint of the Day: A Life and Lesson for Each of the 173 Saints of the New Missal.* Cincinnati, OH: St. Anthony Messenger Press, 1975.

Fraga, Brian, Damian Dovarganes, Olga R. Rodriguez, Michael Sean Winters, Catholic News Service, Cindy Wooden, Pat Marrin, OSV News, Pablo Kay, Sarah Mac Donald, et al. "National Catholic Reporter: The Independent News Source." *National Catholic Reporter | The Independent News Source,* February 20, 2023. https://www.ncronline.org/.

"Saint of the Day Archives." Franciscan Media, 1970. https://www.franciscanmedia.org/saint-of-the-day/.

"Saints Stories for All Ages." Loyola Press, January 19, 2021. https://www.loyolapress.com/catholic-resources/saints/saints-stories-for-all-ages/.

The authors themselves and their own research.

Websites of parishes named after the particular saint.

1. C. S. Lewis, *A Grief Observed* (San Francisco: HarperSanFrancisco, 2001).
2. Elizabeth Ann Seton, *Collected Writings: Volume 1* (Vincent Digital Books, 2000, https://via.library.depaul.edu/vincentian_ebooks/9), 313–314.
3. Ibid., 322.
4. Maya Angelou, *Letter to My Daughter* (New York: Random House, 2008).
5. Nadia Delicata, "'The Talk He Never Gave': Reflections on Marshall McLuhan's 1979 Talk 'Disincarnate Man and the Incarnate Church,'" *Ultimate Reality and Meaning,* vol. 34, nos. 3–4 (2011, published 2015), p. 231.
6. Philip Schaff, "Fathers of the Third Century: Hippolytus, Cyprian, Caius, Novatian," Philip Schaff: Anf05. fathers of the third century: Hippolytus, Cyprian, Caius, Novatian, appendix—christian classics ethereal library, accessed December 12, 2022, https://www.ccel.org/ccel/schaff/anf05.iv.v.vii.html.
7. "St. Perpetua and St. Felicity." Catholic.net, accessed November 14, 2022, https://catholic.net/op/articles/1356/cat/1205/st-perpetua-and-st-felicity.html.
8. Romero spoke these words in a homily entitled "The Church: The Vineyard of the Lord" on October 8, 1978. *Óscar Romero, A Prophetic Bishop Speaks to His People: The Complete Homilies of Archbishop Oscar Arnulfo Romero, vol. 3,* trans. Joseph Owens (Miami: Convivium Press, 2016), 295.
9. Romero spoke these words in a homily entitled "The Three Christian Forces That Will Forge the Liberation of Our People" on November 11, 1979. *Óscar Romero, A Prophetic Bishop Speaks to His People: The Complete Homilies of Archbishop Oscar Arnulfo Romero, vol. 5,* trans. Joseph Owens (Miami: Convivium Press, 2016), 471.
10. Romero spoke these words in an interview with *El Diaro de Caracas* on March 19, 1980, just five days before his assassination. Scott Wright, *Oscar Romero and the Communion of Saints: A Biography* (Maryknoll, NY: Orbis Books, 2009), 131.
11. Ibid., 127.

12. Mmvc61, "Father Hermann Cohen's Mother."

13. Priscilla Throop, "Causes and Cures : The Complete English Translation of *Hildegardis Causae et curae,* vol. 5 / Hildegard of Bingen," 59, 63, 86.

14. Edith Stein, "The Road to Carmel: How I Entered the Carmel in Cologne," *Life of the Spirit (1946–1964),* 4, no. 44 (1950): 365–367. http://www.jstor.org/stable/43703437.

15. *Edith Stein, Life in a Jewish Family: Edith Stein: An Autobiography 1891–1916,* ed. Lucy Gelber and Romaeus Leuven, trans. Josephine Koeppel (Washington, DC: ICS Publications, 2016), 23–25.

16. Edith Stein, *Self-Portrait in Letters, 1916–1942,* trans. Josephine Koeppel, vol. 5 (Washington, DC: ICS Publications, 2016), 82, Google Play.

17. Koeppel, 435.

18. "Wisdom from St. Jane de Chantal," Oblates of St. Francis de Sales, accessed December 6, 2022, https://www.oblates.org/st-jane-wisdom.

19. Ibid.

20. "Year of Faith & St. Jane de Chantal," Visitation Spirit, accessed December 6, 2022, https://visitationspirit.org/2013/01/year-of-faith-st-jane-de-chantal/.

21. Robert Ellsberg, *Blessed Among All Women: Women Saints, Prophets, and Witnesses for Our Time* (Chestnut Ridge, PA: Crossroad, 2007), 289.

22. *Luke (Belief: A Theological Commentary on the Bible)* by Justo Gonzalez, https://www.britannica.com/biography/Saint-Luke.

23. Catherine de Vigri and Marilyn Hall, *The Seven Spiritual Weapons,* trans. Hugh Feiss and Daniela Re (Portland, OR: Wipf and Stock, 2011), 30.

24. David Whyte, *Where Many Rivers Meet* (Langley, WA: Many Rivers Press, 1990).

25. John Chrysostom, *Letters to Saint Olympia,* trans. David C. Ford (Yonkers, NY: St. Vladimir's Seminary Press, 2016), 57, 99.

Stella Maris: copyright © 2023 by Nya Abernathy

St. Madeleine Sophie Barat: copyright © 2023 by Leticia Ochoa Adams

St. Cyprian: copyright © 2023 by Marcie Lynne Alvis-Walker

St. Juan Diego: copyright © 2023 by Karla Mendoza Arana

St. Kevin: copyright © 2023 by Tracy Balzer

St. Oscar Romero: copyright © 2023 by Cameron Bellm

Sts. Perpetua and Felicity: copyright © 2023 by Sara Billups

The Holy Family: copyright © 2023 by Erica Campbell

St. Brigid: copyright © 2023 by Kerry Campbell

St. Martin of Tours: copyright © 2023 by Julie Canlis

St. Teresa of Avila: copyright © 2023 by Madison Chastain

St. Catherine of Alexandria: copyright © 2023 by Christena Cleveland

St. Peregrine: copyright © 2023 by Abby Ellis

St. Mark Ji Tianxiang: copyright © 2023 by Beth Ernest

The Myrrhbearers: copyright © 2023 by Laura Kelly Fanucci

St. Dismas: copyright © 2023 by Elise Crawford Gallagher

St. Bernadette: copyright © 2023 by Jessica Gerhardt

Our Lady of Victory: copyright © 2023 by Alex Gotay, Jr.

St. Luke: copyright © 2023 by Solome Haile

Our Lady Undoer of Knots: copyright © 2023 by Marie Heimann

Madonna and Child: copyright © 2023 by Camille Hernandez

St. Kateri Tekakwitha: copyright © 2023 by Kirby Hoberg

St. Jane Frances de Chantal: copyright © 2023 by Stine Kielsmeier-Cook

St. Catherine of Bologna: copyright © 2023 by Justina Hausmann Kopp

St. Anne: copyright © 2023 by Erin S. Lane

St. Ignatius of Loyola: copyright © 2023 by Father James Martin

Our Lady of Guadalupe: copyright © 2023 by Victoria Mastrangelo

St. Dymphna: copyright © 2023 by D. L. Mayfield

St. Teresa of Calcutta: copyright © 2023 by Rakhi McCormick

Sts. Priscilla and Aquilla: copyright © 2023 by India Jade McCue

St. Zoe: copyright © 2023 by Cara Meredith

St. Christopher: copyright © 2023 by Gracie Morbitzer

St. Simeon Stylites the Younger: copyright © 2023 by Gracie Morbitzer

St. Mary MacKillop: copyright © 2023 by Isabel Morbitzer

St. Thérèse of Lisieux: copyright © 2023 by Jennifer Nutzman

St. Monica: copyright © 2023 by Tsh Oxenreider

St. Paul: copyright © 2023 by Ryan J. Pelton

St. Elizabeth Ann Seton: copyright © 2023 by Margaret Philpot

St. Junia: copyright © 2023 by Jenny Booth Potter

St. Brendan: copyright © 2023 by Sarah Quint

St. Olympias: copyright © 2023 by Renée Roden

St. Elizabeth of Hungary: copyright © 2023 by Kristin Victoria Sancken

The Visitation: copyright © 2023 by Kelly Sankowski

St. Martha: copyright © 2023 by Shannon W. Schmidt

St. Edith Stein: copyright © 2023 by Corynne Staresinic

The New Eve: copyright © 2023 by Morgan Strehlow

St. John the Baptist: copyright © 2023 by Sarah Bond Strong

St. Zélie: copyright © 2023 by Clare Swinarski

Sts. Sergius and Bacchus: copyright © 2023 by Theo Swinford

St. Hildegard of Bingen: copyright © 2023 by Meghan Tschanz

St. John: copyright © 2023 by Laura Eve Tushnet

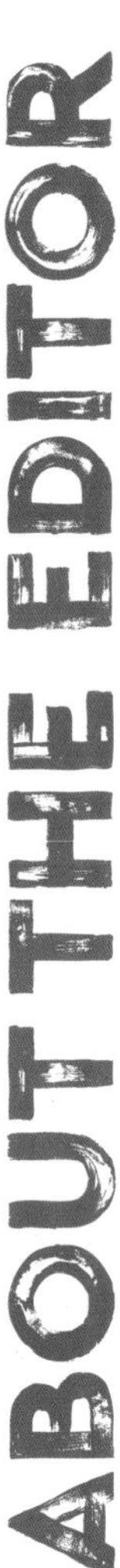

Gracie Morbitzer (she/her) is the artist and business owner behind the project The Modern Saints. She works in Columbus, Ohio, and is part of the Franklinton artist community. She enjoys exploring all types of creative mediums and writing and loves to travel. She lives with her beloveds, Sam and Tater Tot, in downtown Columbus.

Themodernsaints.com
themodernsaints@yahoo.com
Instagram: @the_modern_saints_by_gracie
Facebook.com/TheModernSaintsbyGracie